QUINCES

To

Bill, Sophie and Rose

THE ENGLISH KITCHEN

QUINCES

GROWING AND COOKING

JANE McMORLAND HUNTER
AND
SUE DUNSTER

PROSPECT BOOKS
2014

This edition published in 2014 by Prospect Books at 26 Parke Road, London, SW13 9NG
Reprinted 2015 (twice), 2018, 2023.

British Library Cataloguing in Publication Data:
A catalogue entry for this book is available from the British Library.

ISBN 978-1-909248-41-0

Printed by the Short Run Press, Exeter, United Kingdom.

TABLE OF CONTENTS

Introduction   7

The Story of the Quince   9

Quinces in the Garden   20

Quinces in the Kitchen   36
    Baked quinces   41
    Poached quinces   44
    Preserves   52
    Savoury dishes   60
    Sweet dishes   71
    Afternoon tea   85
    Drinks and liqueurs   91
    Confectionery   97

The Books that Made Quinces Popular   103

The Lost World of the Quince: Health and Beauty   119

Acknowledgements   123

Bibliography   124

Index   126

INTRODUCTION

O ut of season quinces are impossible to obtain and even in season they are usually only available at the more inspired farmers' markets and a few selective shops. This seems a sorry state of affairs for a fruit which is delicious in both sweet and savoury dishes, can easily be preserved and will enhance a room with an unmistakable yet delicate fragrance.

The easy solution is to grow your own quinces and the purpose of this book is to encourage everyone to do exactly that. Quinces grow on attractive trees which never become unmanageably large and will improve any garden. They can even be grown in containers. In late spring the trees are covered with the most exquisite, fragrant blossom. This ranges from white to pale pink and is set against a backdrop of furry grey-green leaves. The blossom does not last long, but while it is in flower there is little that can rival it. The trees themselves grow in a twisty, slightly mad, but attractive manner, although some varieties can be trained against a wall in an espalier or fan. The fruit appears in late summer and ripens towards the end of autumn. In northern Europe the fruit never ripens sufficiently to be eaten raw, but is so delicious once cooked that this really does not matter. The trees are highly productive and fairly unfussy as to where they grow, in particular, the cultivar 'Meech's Prolific' certainly lives up to its name. The trees self-pollinate which means you only need one to get fruit. They are largely disease free, fruit reliably most years and will live to a great age, enhancing your garden and providing you with a scrumptious crop in return for little input.

Quinces were reputed to be the fruit which Paris gave Aphrodite and it was said that quince trees grew up wherever she walked. They may have been the infamous fruits on the Tree of Wisdom in the Garden of Eden. Much later Edward Lear's Owl and Pussycat dined on them at their wedding feast. They originally came to Europe from central Asia where they still grow wild in the foothills of the Caucasus Mountains in Turkmenistan and Iran. They have been used in Persian cooking for over 2,500 years, but probably reached Britain in the thirteenth century where they appear in recipes for pies sweetened with honey.

Quinces are deliciously sweet and scented when cooked. They contain a high level of pectin and can therefore easily be made into jams and jellies. Originally marmalade was made from quinces coming from the Portuguese word for the fruit, *marmelo*. A little goes a long way and the addition of a few slices will transform sweet and savoury dishes. They combine particularly well with apples and pears, but will also go with almonds, oranges and even mulberries, if you can get them. They can be made into cakes, tarts, biscuits and custards. They are used in many Mediterranean and central Asian savoury dishes including chicken, pork and all types of game. They can be stuffed with meat and used to flavour savoury tarts. There is so much more to them than just the jelly and *membrillo* commonly found in delicatessens.

Even before you cook with them quinces can be used to scent a room. Once ripened, they are an attractive golden colour and will keep in a bowl giving off a delightful fragrance.

The first part of this book gives a brief history of quinces to put them into context in both the kitchen and the garden. A section on growing quince trees follows which gives all the information you need to select and care for a suitable cultivar. The final part covers storing, cooking and using the fruit, in both modern and historic recipes. Do not be put off by the fact that they usually need to be cooked, so do lots of other ingredients and the rewards for cooking quinces are enormous.

THE STORY OF THE QUINCE

The earliest known quinces grew wild in the foothills of the Caucasus Mountains between Persia and Turkmenistan. This seemingly inhospitable area is actually very fertile and many fruits thrived. A knobbly, irregular-shaped variety still grows wild in this area. The valleys below formed many of the ancient trade routes and quinces spread rapidly westwards and eastwards. To the west they were carried along the old trade routes, reaching the Middle East and then the Mediterranean as Golden Apples, flourishing as they went. To the east they were taken across the deserts of the Silk Road and thence to China where they arrived as the Golden Peaches of Samarkand.

They quickly became very popular and were credited with both mythical and medicinal powers. From ancient times right up to the late Middle Ages quinces were, in most places, more widely used and better known than apples. Related to both apples and pears, it is sometimes hard to identify quinces in classical literature, especially as the Greeks tended to use the term *melon* to refer to both apples and quinces, but it is likely that most golden apples mentioned were actually quinces as they would have been more widely cultivated and better known, particularly in the Levant and southern Europe. It is important to remember that the quinces of central Asia, the Middle East and south America can often be eaten straight from the tree. Quinces were also favoured because it is only comparatively recently that the people of the West have developed such a sweet tooth. Many other regions of the world still appreciate astringent flavours and historically these tastes would have been the norm as sweeteners other than honey were rare and expensive.

One of the quince's earliest possible claims to fame is the Judgement of Paris in Greek mythology. Eris is the Greek goddess of strife and in a foolish miscalculation she was the only god not invited to the wedding of Peleus and Thetis. Understandably furious, she barged into the wedding ceremony and threw down a fruit inscribed 'For the most beautiful.' This fruit was described as a golden apple and was, almost certainly, a quince. Hera, Athene and Aphrodite each claimed the fruit, so Zeus decided that the matter should be settled by Paris. Hera offered him empire, Athene guaranteed military glory and Aphrodite promised him the most beautiful woman in the world. This was Helen, who was unfortunately already married to Menelaus of Sparta. Paris gave the fruit to Aphrodite and she in turn helped him win Helen, thereby sparking off the Trojan War. The main result of this episode for quinces is that ever after they have been regarded as Aphrodite's fruit. They are associated with love and fertility and it was believed that the trees sprang up wherever she walked, alongside the better known flowers.

The quince's link with Aphrodite ensured it an unofficial place in wedding ceremonies. In 594 BC Solon was elected chief magistrate of Athens. He was a politician, but also a poet and although he is described by George Forrest in *The Oxford History of the Classical World* as being 'self-centred, self-righteous and just a trifle pompous' he at least kept written records and concerned himself with more than simply amassing power. He tried to establish peace and democracy by writing a new law code and instituting social and political reforms. In due course he set down the format for wedding ceremonies and the quince's part was officially recorded. From then on quinces have been part of the Greek wedding ceremony and are often baked in a cake with honey and sesame seeds. This is said to symbolize the couple's enduring commitment to each other through good times and bad. The fruits are often thrown to the bride and groom as they go to their new home and the bride is presented with a quince to ensure fertility. One myth says that pregnant women who indulge their appetites in generous quantities of quince will give birth to industrious and highly intelligent children. Edward

Lear was following an ancient precedent when he included quinces in the Owl and the Pussy-cat's wedding feast.

The Owl and the Pussy-cat went to sea
In a beautiful pea-green boat,
They took some honey, and plenty of money,
Wrapped up in a five-pound note.
The Owl looked up to the stars above,
And sang to a small guitar,
'O lovely Pussy! O Pussy my love,
What a beautiful Pussy you are
You are,
You are!
What a beautiful Pussy you are!'
Pussy said to the Owl 'You elegant fowl!
How charmingly sweet you sing!
O let us be married! Too long we have tarried:
But what shall we do for a ring?'
They sailed away, for a year and a day
To the land where the Bong-tree grows
And there in a wood a Piggy-wig stood
With a ring at the end of his nose,
His nose,
His nose,
With a ring at the end of his nose.

'Dear Pig, are you willing to sell for one shilling
Your ring?' Said the Piggy 'I will.'
So they took it away, and were married next day
By the Turkey who lives on the hill.
They dined on mince and slices of quince
Which they ate with a runcible spoon;
And hand in hand, on the edge of the sand,
They danced by the light of the moon,
The moon,
The moon,
They danced by the light of the moon.

(Edward Lear (1812–1888), *Nonsense Verse*)

Golden apples or quinces also feature in the myth of the twelve tasks of Heracles. As the eleventh task he had to fetch the fruit from the golden apple tree in Hera's sacred garden on the slopes of Mount Atlas. The tree had been Mother Earth's wedding gift to Hera and she had created her divine garden around it. Guarded by the dragon Ladon and surrounded by a high wall, scrumping from the garden was clearly a formidable task. Ladon was curled round the base of the tree and Heracles had to shoot him with an arrow, before persuading Atlas to fetch the fruit. This proved surprisingly easy, as Atlas was carrying the globe on his shoulders and Heracles offered to support it for him in return for the fruit. This was a popular tale for sculptors and artists and the scene of Heracles supporting the world while Atlas brings him the golden apples can be seen on a white-ground vase in the National Archaeological Museum in Athens. On this vase the fruits do look remarkably knobbly, giving further support to the idea that they were actually quinces, rather than apples. There is also a splendid statue of Heracles in the British Museum in London, showing him standing in front of the tree with three golden apples in his hand. Again, the fruits could easily be quinces, rather than apples.

There are records of quinces being cultivated 5,000 years ago by the Mesopotamians and from 100 BC onwards they were popular in Palestine long before apples. It is quite likely that the fruit in both the Garden of Eden and the Song of Solomon were quinces rather than apples.

The Romans also cultivated quinces, particularly for their medicinal qualities. There is a terracotta quince in the British Museum which is over two thousand years old. It was made in Apulia in southern Italy between 300 and 250 BC and was obviously originally part of a collection as a pomegranate has also survived. The fruit is life size and you can really see the knobbliness. Cato, in his farming manual of 202 BC, *On Agriculture,* included a number of recipes and recommended growing three types of quince: *Strutea, Cotonea* and *Mustea,* a variety which ripened well. Pliny, a Roman naturalist in the first century AD, praised their medicinal virtues, claiming, among other things, that they warded off the evil eye. He mentions the *Mulvan* variety, which was the only cultivated quince at the time that could be eaten raw. Quinces also featured in *The Satyricon,* by Petronius. Written around 65 AD this was a huge work of which only a small part survives. It is an amusing literary portrait of Roman society at the time and follows the adventures of two scholars as they wander through the cities of the Mediterranean. In Rome they go to a dinner given by Trimalchio, a vulgar freedman who has considerably more money than style. The whole event becomes more and more tasteless, culminating with a dessert including 'Quinces, with thorns implanted to make them look like sea urchins.' It is not clear whether this dish is actually eaten, but quince dishes were obviously well known enough for Petronius to use them in his book. The Greeks and Romans preserved quinces in honey, giving rise to the name *melimelum* from the Greek for honey apple. In turn this evolved into the Spanish *marmello* and thence *membrillo* which is probably the best known use for quinces nowadays.

An early use for quinces which has now largely vanished was marmalade. Many fruits contain pectin, which allows them to set as jam or jelly when cooked. This quality was first discovered in quinces by the Romans, who cooked the fruit prior to preserving it. Quinces were the only fruits that needed cooking first and for a long time it was assumed that they were the only fruits that would set in this way. The resulting conserve was popular on the Continent and came to

Britain in the sixteenth century via Portugal as *marmelada,* from the Portuguese for quinces, *marmelo.* It was expensive and recipes soon began appearing in British recipe books, again only using quinces. Similar preserves had been made since Roman times, but it is only with the arrival of *marmelada* that they become really popular. The name soon became marmalade and until the eighteenth century this usually meant a conserve made with quinces. Gradually, other fruits were used and over time oranges or citrus fruits were used for marmalade and other fruits for jams or conserves. Britain is the only European country to make this distinction; elsewhere *marmelada* and related words refer to fruit preserves of all types.

The Greeks themselves were always great quince producers and developed a variety which was superior to the traditional *Strythion.* It came from the Minoan port of Kydonia or Cydonia (now Chania) in Crete and although the fruit was smaller and more astringent it had more flavour. Gradually the name for all quinces changed from *Strythion* to *Cydonia* and this is the Latin name by which tree quinces are now known, to distinguish them from the flowering or Japanese varieties (*Chaenomeles*). The original Latin term for the fruit was *cotoneum* and this, in turn, has evolved into the French *coin* or *coings.* In England in the Middle Ages the Old French name *coyn* or *quoyn* was used but by the fourteenth century the words had merged and the name quince was widespread.

Quinces probably travelled to Britain from France where they were widespread. The Emperor Charlemagne may not have introduced them to the region but he certainly recognized their value, as demonstrated by his order, in 812, that they were to be planted in the royal garden. They certainly grew in more southerly climes and it is from early medieval times that one of the only poems exclusively about quinces dates. Its author was Shafer ben Utman al-Mushafi, vizier to Caliph Al-Hakam II of Cordoba in Andalusia until his death in 982. The poem was rediscovered by the Spanish scholar Emilio García Lopez in 1928 and this translation by A.L. Lloyd was one of the many fine and apposite quotations included by the late Jane Grigson in her *Fruit Book* of 1982.

It is yellow in colour, as if it wore a daffodil
tunic, and it smells like musk, a penetrating smell.

It has the perfume of a loved woman and the same
hardness of heart, but it has the colour of the
impassioned and scrawny lover.

Its pallor is borrowed from my pallor; its smell
is my sweetheart's breath.

When it stood fragrant on the bough and the leaves
had woven for it a covering of brocade,

I gently put up my hand to pluck it and set it
like a censer in the middle of my room.

It had a cloak of ash-coloured down hovering over
its smooth golden body,

and when it lay naked in my hand, with nothing more than
its daffodil-coloured shift,

it made me think of her I cannot mention, and I feared
the ardour of my breath would shrivel it in my fingers.

Quinces were first recorded in England in 1275 when King Edward
I planted four at the Tower of London. It is possible that he was
influenced in this by the *Dictionarius* of John of Garland which had
been written in 1250. This provided an inventory of a good Parisian
garden and included quinces as one of the required fruits. The trees
planted at the Tower cost sixpence each. A modern equivalent is
hardly possible, but think £15. In 1292 more trees were planted at
Westminster. These were priced at forty-one shillings for 100 (think
more than £1,000), which is cheaper per sapling, but the variation may
simply be due to the bulk purchase. Chaucer mentions them, using

the term *coines*, a variation of the French *coings*. They were certainly well known in England by the fourteenth century, with cookery books including recipes for quince pies and preserves. From then until the end of the nineteenth century quinces feature more prominently than apples in most English cookery books. They make fewer appearances in Scottish books, but this is possibly because the trees were associated with the warmer climates of southern Europe and were considered too delicate to survive. Most people were probably unaware that the trees originally came from considerably colder regions in central Asia.

Quinces rapidly gained popularity in the Middle Ages. They were easy to preserve and, as well as being delicious, they were credited with a number of medicinal qualities. The fact that they had to be cooked did not matter, as raw fruit was regarded with suspicion and felt to be potentially dangerous to one's health. This was largely based on the fact that when there was a glut people tended to overeat and make themselves ill. Fresh fruit was not really regarded as safe until the eighteenth century and till then the prudent way to eat it was to cook it first with sugar and spices to preserve it, or make a purée which could then be baked in pies. Quinces' popularity was further increased as, along with oranges and pomegranates, they were regarded as protection against plagues in general and the Black Death in particular. Quince paste, or chardequynce as it became known in England, featured at the end of many meals as it was attractive, tasted good and did you good. The paste was frequently set in moulds and could be gilded for special occasions. This paste was also called cotoniak or paste of Genoa, with quiddony or quiddoniak referring to a translucent jelly which was similar. In France it was called *cotignac*, with the best being *Cotignac d'Orleans*. This was boiled with sugar to form a clear jelly which was an attractive ruby colour. It was then poured into small round wooden boxes to set. These were often presented to visiting royalty when they passed through outlying towns and villages. In 1429 Joan of Arc was presented with a gift of *cotignac* when she arrived at Orleans to liberate it from the English. Ever since, *cotignac* has been made in moulds of her likeness.

Medieval cooks at the highest levels in royal and aristocratic households undoubtedly had a reasonable knowledge of the other characteristics of each dish as well as its taste. Remedies and festival recipes had close links and the cooks would have ensured that the humours of the various foods matched. It was considered important that the four humours (sanguine, phlegmatic, choleric and melancholic) were balanced within a meal and although this wasn't particularly scientific it did make rough sense and most medieval banquets were actually quite well balanced and nutritious even by today's standards. For their medicinal qualities, quinces were frequently included at the end of banquets.

The menu from the coronation of Richard III in 1483 survives and the last named dish on it is 'Quynces Bake.' The recipe states that the quinces should be cored, filled with sugar and ginger and baked in a pastry coffin. Quinces and ginger went together well and were both regarded as aids to digestion. Sugar was felt to be good for the stomach and so this would have been an ideal end to a heavy feast. (See page 42 for a modern variation of this recipe.)

The Tudor aphrodisiacs, in the recipe section on page 97, would have offered much the same benefits to the digestion – with the added advantage of helping in bed later on in the evening. Quince marmalade was regarded as an aphrodisiac and often had almonds added to encourage fertility. Its reputation in Tudor times was so great that it was served to Queen Mary, who was desperate to conceive a son once she had achieved the throne in 1554 and married Philip of Spain. Unfortunately, it failed, and although the reputation persisted, the status of marmalade fell somewhat during the seventeenth century if the equivalence of 'marmulet madams' with prostitutes is any guide. In 1727 Edward Ward remarked 'More marmulet madams will be met strolling in the fields than honest women.'

Another sixteenth-century queen, Mary, Queen of Scots, also used quinces, but this time to combat seasickness when crossing from Calais to Scotland in 1561. Quinces were long regarded not only as an aid to digestion but also as a prevention against sickness. In 1579 William Langham wrote in *The Garden of Health* that marmalade 'is very good to strengthen the stomach and to keep the meat therein till it be perfectly digested.'

Throughout the seventeenth and eighteenth centuries quinces remained popular in Britain, being added to pies and tarts and made into sauces to accompany game. John Parkinson, botanist to King Charles II, said 'there is no fruit growing in the land that is of so many excellent uses as this, serving well to make many dishes of meat for the table, as for banquets, and much more for their physical virtues'. 'Quynces Bake' still appeared at banquets and was reputed to be a favourite dish of Sir Isaac Newton. In 1611 John Tradescant had imported the 'Portingall' or 'Portugal', which has remained one of the best varieties up to the present day (it is now usually known as 'Lusitanica'). By the middle of the seventeenth century demand outstripped supply and quinces were imported from Flanders. At this time it was common to store quinces for as long as two years in a barrel, submerged in perry or ale. Periodically the alcohol could be removed and drunk and the fruit topped up with fresh alcohol, as necessary.

Popular as they were, quinces rarely featured in literature. Juliet's nurse mentions that quinces will be eaten at the wedding feast, but Shakespeare's most famous quince, Peter Quince, the carpenter in *A Midsummer Night's Dream,* sadly has nothing to do with the fruit. His name derives from *quines* or *quoins,* the wedges which carpenters use to steady the pieces they are cutting.

By the nineteenth century, the balance had changed and there was such a surplus of quinces in Sussex that the fruit was made into wine. This was partly because horticultural methods had improved, but also because the quince was beginning to lose its status as more soft fruit was grown.

In North America there were no native quinces, but they were introduced by the European settlers and by 1720 they were thriving in Virginia. Here the Reverend W.W. Meech raised a variety which is still grown today: 'Meech's Prolific', a tree which lives up to its name. Gradually they spread south and became extremely popular in Latin America where in some areas they had been introduced directly by Spanish and Portuguese settlers. Here they were eaten raw, partly because the climate produced sweeter fruit and also because the population was used to more astringent tastes. Today, some of the largest commercial quince plantations are in Paraguay where the trees do well.

By the beginning of the twentieth century quinces had lost much of their allure and mystery. With the decline of servants and the quickening pace of life they were increasingly regarded as too much bother to cook and so fell out of favour. The trees were still planted in gardens, but as a result of the plant-hunters in Victorian times so many more species were available to gardeners and orchardists and, with the wider choice, the trees also became scarcer. In the twenty-first century the assumption that quick is best has been questioned and a new emphasis on home-grown produce has meant that many old varieties are coming back into favour. It is to be hoped that quinces will benefit from these changes.

QUINCES IN THE GARDEN

A hundred years ago quince trees would have been found in almost every orchard in Britain. They would have been considered on a par with apples, pears and plums and grown in both commercial orchards and domestic gardens. The fruit then fell out of favour, but increasingly quinces are regaining their position as popular fruit trees.

They are an attractive addition to almost any garden, regardless of size. They have beautiful blossom in spring, followed by glossy leaves which start off a pale grey-green in spring and during summer develop into a dark green, with felty white undersides. These then turn attractive shades of yellow and brown in autumn. Quinces naturally grow into bushy trees, with interestingly contorted branches that look attractive even when bare in winter.

The fragrant blossom consists of little, pale pink flowers similar to a dog rose. The buds are varying shades of pink, some striped, like a barber's pole. As the flowers open fully they fade until they are almost pure white. The fruit grows on the tree towards the end of summer and looks particularly lovely as it turns from pale green to rich golden yellow, with a furry grey coat. The fruits themselves are usually pear-shaped and give off a sweet fragrance as they ripen. As an added bonus the spring blossom will attract beneficial insects to your garden and if you leave a few fruits on the trees they will provide winter food for birds and squirrels.

As well as all this, the trees are reasonably disease-free and are easy to look after. There is also a certain romance about quinces, with their myths, legends and illustrious history. Robin Lane Fox writes a wonderful description of their arrival in China: 'I like to think of its first arrival from central Asia in the exquisite circles of Tang China, where it would have accompanied the dances and new music, furs, jewellery and radical religions which burst on Chinese society from their source in the distant West. Away beyond the White Dragon Dunes and the Mountains of Heaven lay the home of the Golden Peaches.' As he then says, 'The thought sustains one's interest in a quince tree even when it has lost its leaves.'

FAMILY

Quinces were originally thought of as a type of pear and were first called *Pyrus cydonia,* or the Cydonian pear. Later they were given a separate classification and are now properly called *Cydonia oblonga.* They are sometimes called tree quinces to distinguish them from *Chaenomeles* or the flowering quince, which is again a separate plant. Flowering quinces are usually grown as shrubs or climbers. Their blossom comes in a huge range of colours from white to orange to deep crimson. The fruits are edible, but are really only suitable for jelly. The two quinces are distantly related, both belonging to the rose family, *Rosaceae,* but for the beautiful trees and a delicious crop for the kitchen, it is *Cydonia* that you need.

SITE

Quinces come from the foothills of the Caucasus Mountains, a region with long, hot summers and harsh winters. They are fully hardy and will grow anywhere in Britain. Our fruits may not be as large as those grown in the Middle East or central Asia, but they are still delicious and the trees will thrive anywhere from Inverary in Scotland to Faversham in Kent.

Ideally the trees like a long, hot summer, but also need a cold spell in winter. They become dormant in the autumn to protect the new growth and then need about 400 hours of temperatures below 7°C to break the dormancy. If they do not get this the blossom (and the resulting harvest) will be delayed or poor. Quinces can easily tolerate temperatures as low as -26°C, but do not particularly like long periods of cold, damp weather or harsh winds. For this reason they grow particularly well against south-facing walls or in the sheltered corners of walled gardens. As the trees flower in late spring, frost is not usually a problem, a chilly wind can do far more harm.

If you have a sheltered garden and sufficient space, quince trees look particularly lovely grown in the middle of a lawn where their rounded, umbrella shape can fully develop. They look equally good grown in a small courtyard and will even thrive in a pot as long as it is sufficiently large and you tend the plant well. One of the great advantages of quince trees is that they are self-fertile, so you should get a reasonable crop of fruit even if you only have one tree.

An orchard of quince trees or even a mixed orchard is a fantastic thing to create. It will start providing you with fruit a couple of years after you have planted the trees and will quickly develop into a beautiful part of the garden. Early monasteries always had orchards, often with quinces predominating. Surprisingly, you don't need that much space or even that many trees to create the feel of an orchard. You could grow quinces, apples, pears and even cobnuts and medlars. Just ensure that the site is sheltered and has reasonably good, well drained soil. Plant the trees as you would for individual specimens below, allowing a few feet between each tree and wait for your harvest!

BUYING

Quinces often do not fruit for the first four or five years so there is no great advantage in buying a particularly young tree. It is best to buy two-year-old bushes or three- or four-year-old trees so that the basic shape is already formed for you. This is particularly important if you want to fan-train the plant against a wall.

The size of the tree will be governed by the rootstock. Most fruit trees do not grow true from seed and all the quinces you buy in nurseries will have been grafted onto a rootstock which will grow to a predetermined size. Quince A is the most common stock, giving a tree about 4.5 metres (15 feet) tall and is often described as semi-vigorous. This is the most suitable for growing trees and fan or espalier shapes. Quince C is a semi-dwarfing rootstock, giving trees reaching 3 metres

(10 feet) in height. It is the most suitable for growing in containers, although it is not as tough as Quince A and needs good soil and a sheltered site. EMH is a less common rootstock, is between the other two in size, and is much more robust than Quince C. Always check the rootstock when buying a tree, it is as important as the upper part, which will determine the actual fruit.

The trees are self-fertile but you will probably get a slightly better crop if you grow two cultivars. The best advice is probably to grow more than one tree if you have the space, but don't worry if you only have room for one as you will still get fruit.

TREES FROM SEED

Most people buy established plants from a nursery, but it is perfectly possible to grow your own trees from seed. This will take several years and you need to bear in mind that quinces, like apples, do not grow 'true' from seed. There is no guarantee what sort of quince you will get or, perhaps more importantly, how large it will grow, as it will not be on a predetermined rootstock. You might eventually end up with a monster tree bearing little or no fruit! You can also take cuttings from an existing tree, but again, it is safer to buy your plant from a reputable nursery.

PLANTING

Quince trees are shallow rooted and need a rich, moist soil which does not become waterlogged in winter or dry out in summer. A neutral or slightly acid pH is best but the trees are not really that fussy.

Bare-rooted plants should be moved during the dormant period between November and March. Container-grown plants can be put in at any time. Dig a hole large enough to accommodate the root ball easily and position the tree so that the scion (graft join) is at least 100 mm / 4 inches above the surrounding soil. This will ensure that your tree will grow to the size indicated by the rootstock. Backfill the hole and push the soil down gently but firmly. The trees should be staked to allow the stems to grow strongly, as quinces tend to be top heavy. You can leave the stake there permanently, as long as the ties don't cut into the bark. Put a layer of mulch (well rotted farmyard manure or compost) around the base of the tree, leaving a gap immediately around the trunk to prevent the wood becoming soggy. The mulch will provide nutrients for the tree and stop the soil drying out too fast. This is particularly important on light sandy soils.

If you are planting several trees, or even an orchard, you should place the trees so that there will be a gap between each one when they are fully grown. Taking the cultivar and rootstock into consideration, work out the final spread of each tree and allow a few feet extra between each one. There may seem to be a lot of space when you first put the plants in but a decent gap will ensure that none of your plants are competing against one another for nutrients or sunlight.

CARE

A real advantage to quince trees over other orchard fruits is that, once established, they require little attention. For the first three years you should aim to water regularly, ensuring that the soil remains damp but does not become soggy. Check that the plant is growing into the shape you want and that none of the ties or stakes are rubbing against any of the stems.

You should mulch every spring once the soil has warmed up. Garden compost or well rotted manure are the best mulches as they will nourish the plant, improve the soil structure and provide a protective layer which will prevent water evaporating and deter weeds. Bark chips are one of the most easily available mulches and although they have no nutritional value they look attractive, will prevent water evaporation and, if you buy partly composted chips, they will quickly break down and improve the soil. Spread the mulch in a 50 mm/2 inch layer over the ground, covering roughly the same area as the branches above. This will ensure the area over the roots is covered. Leave a gap between the mulch and the trunk to prevent the wood rotting.

Whether your plant is freestanding or trained against a wall it will benefit from a feed in late winter or early spring. If you mulch with garden compost or well rotted manure you will be providing this

food, but if you use anything else you need to give the plant a feed of general fertilizer, such as organic seaweed. Apply this over an area of soil roughly the same as the tree branches so the area of the roots is covered. This will encourage the tree to spread its roots right out which will make it healthier and more stable.

Quinces bruise incredibly easily and can be damaged just by rubbing against an adjoining fruit on the tree. These bruises are not always visible on the surface. Thin the fruits when they are still small so that they do not jostle against one another. This will give you a better harvest of good fruit in the autumn and removing the excess weight will prevent the branches sagging.

GROWING IN CONTAINERS

Quince trees can be successfully grown in containers although they will never reach the size of freely growing plants and will need extra care throughout their lives. Buy a two- to three-year-old container-grown plant on Quince C rootstock. Use a pot which is at least 600 mm / 2 feet deep and the same width. Obviously the larger the pot the healthier and happier the tree will be, so go for the largest one you can fit in your garden. Make sure the pot has holes at the bottom to allow excess water to soak away and put a 50 mm/2-inch layer of broken crocks in the bottom to help drainage. Use specialist peat-free shrub compost which will provide the necessary starter nutrients for the plant. The nutrients in these composts rarely last more than a few months (check the bag to see exactly how long they will sustain the plant for) and after that you will need to feed the plant regularly. Leave a 50 mm/2-inch gap between the top of the pot and the surface of the soil. This will allow you to add a good layer of mulch each spring. Remove the fruit in the first year so the plant can concentrate on establishing itself. Thereafter feed with a general supplement during the growing season and water regularly so that the soil remains damp but not soggy.

PRUNING AND TRAINING

Quince trees can be trained flat against a wall, but you have to start at an early age because of their naturally twisty growth. You need to aim to create an even spread of main stems with short, productive branches growing out from them. Remember that the main stems will not remain productive indefinitely so you need to keep a supply of shorter stems ready to train out. This sounds easy in theory, but in practice your quince will probably not prove so obliging. The young shoots are quite pliable but you will need to check every couple of months to ensure the plant spreads out properly. Fix the stems to a firm framework such as strong wires or trellis. Use soft garden twine as this will hold the branches in place but will not damage them as they grow. After the first three years the basic framework will be established and you will just need to follow the general pruning guidelines below. The advantage of fan or espalier training is that the tree will take up very little space and will flower and crop well against a sunny wall. If you want to do this it is best to buy a partially trained tree from a specialist nursery.

For freestanding trees a goblet shape is best as this allows light and air through the tree and is reasonably easy to maintain. For the first 4–5 years you should cut back the leaders of the main framework branches by half the previous summer's growth. Side shoots should be cut back to 2–3 buds. Remember to find out how old your tree is when you buy it as you do not want to carry out this formative pruning for longer than necessary.

After the initial formation, pruning is fairly simple and is best carried out on a 'little and often' basis. You want to maximize the amount of fruit and maintain the shape of the tree and for the health of the plant you should avoid doing anything too drastic. Remember that the trees bear blossom (and fruit) on the spurs and tips of the previous summer's growth so you should only remove what is absolutely necessary. Pruning should be carried out in winter when the tree is dormant. Suckers round the base should be cut away, as should any shoots which appear on the clear part of the trunk. This will establish a good, open framework for your tree and after that it should not need too much ongoing pruning. Remove any dead or weak stems and in particular cut away any stems which start to grow crosswise into the middle of the plant. This keeps the tree open so it gets plenty of light and ventilation which will prevent disease and help the fruit ripen. At Norton Priory, where they have the National Collection of quinces, the aim is to be able to throw your hat through the centre of the tree in winter. If you have an open fire keep the prunings as they make brilliant kindling.

PESTS AND DISEASES

If well looked after, quince trees should be comparatively free of pests and diseases. Leaf blight, which is caused by a fungus, can be a problem. It causes speckled leaves, defoliation and, if severe, fruit loss. It appears in early summer with small spots on the leaves which are reddish at first and then turn black. The spots themselves are not large (about 4 millimetres or one eighth of an inch across) but may join up to form larger patches. In severe cases the shoots may stop growing. The fruit which does grow tends to be affected, with roughened skins and cracks which allow brown rot to develop. There is no chemical cure, but otherwise healthy plants should be able to withstand an attack. Remove any affected leaves, mulch round the base and keep well watered. In autumn rake up and dispose of all the fallen leaves.

This is most important as the fungus can survive the winter amongst fallen debris and will re-infect the plant the following spring. When pruning in the winter, cut away any badly infected branches. If you are worried grow resistant varieties such as 'Vranja' or 'Portugal' and avoid 'Champion', which is the most susceptible.

Aphids, coddling moth, slugworm or caterpillars may attack the fruit but are not usually a serious problem. Since you are going to eat the fruit it seems pointless to spray it with a mass of chemicals; the best way is to keep a regular eye on the fruit so you can spot any infestation and deal with it before it becomes a problem. Spray any aphids with a weak solution of organic washing-up liquid or liquid seaweed, pick off any caterpillars and remove any eaten fruit. Birds and squirrels are unlikely to be a problem as the fruit is so hard that they tend to leave it alone until everything else in the garden has gone, by which time you will have harvested everything you want. Mice can be a nuisance, but they do not usually eat much of the crop.

The only disease which can be a problem is Apple Powdery Mildew. This only occurs when the tree is planted in dry soil and, as with most plant diseases, prevention is really better than cure. If you know your soil has a tendency to dry out, mix in lots of organic matter before planting and add a layer of mulch at least 50 mm / 2 inches deep every spring. If your tree does develop the disease you will notice a white, powdery growth on the leaves. The leaves will drop early and the fruit may also be affected. Cut away and destroy any diseased parts, keep the plant well watered and mulch well the following year to prevent the problem recurring.

HARVESTING AND STORING

The ideal way to harvest quinces is to leave them on the trees for as long as possible, but to remove them before the first frost. If the fruit is frosted it will not keep so well. As with most tree fruit, quinces are ready to pick if they come away when gently twisted. The beauty of the ripening process is that it is naturally staggered and you will be able to harvest throughout the autumn.

Be very careful when collecting the fruit as it spoils much more easily than you would expect. Dropping them carelessly into a basket will almost certainly cause bruising and make the fruit more likely to rot. For the same reason windfalls need to be used immediately.

Quinces will keep for a couple of months if unblemished. Put them on trays and store in a cool, airy place; a garden shed is ideal if you have one. Lay the fruits so they do not touch one another, this way it won't matter if one starts to rot. You can simply remove the damaged fruit and the surrounding fruit will be unaffected. You can buy attractive trays which will stack neatly, but just as good are the simple slatted trays you will find for virtually nothing at most markets. In the Middle Ages it was common to lay the quinces on a bed of ashes from the hearth to protect them and in the nineteenth century quinces were stored in trays lined with poplar or pine sawdust. Any of these would have kept the fruit dry and cushioned, but they aren't really necessary.

Stored quinces can give off a heady aroma which will be a blessing or a curse, according to your attitude. Mrs Beeton in her *Household Management* was clearly not impressed: 'This fruit has the remarkable peculiarity of exhaling an agreeable odour, taken singly, but when in any quantity, or when they are stowed away in a drawer or close room, the pleasant aroma becomes an intolerable stench, although the fruit may be perfectly sound; it is therefore desirable that, as but a few quinces are required for keeping, they should be kept in a high and dry loft, and out of the way of the rooms used by the family.' Many Victorian household manuals suggest storing quinces in flat trays at the top of the linen cupboard where they will scent your laundry. The point to be wary of is that they will scent any other fruit stored with them. Apples and pears mix well with quinces in cooking but you do not want them smelling of quinces at the start if you want to use them in separate dishes. Do not be tempted to store the quinces in plastic bags. The fruit will appear fine, but will tend to discolour on the inside. Quinces can also be preserved in jars, cooked or frozen and this is covered in the next chapter.

WHICH QUINCE TO PLANT?

Most quinces grow to a roughly similar size and shape and their fruit is often indistinguishable. Fruit specialists such as Brogdale at Faversham in Kent or the National Collection at Norton Priory in Cheshire each have around twenty cultivars, but in reality your choice may be restricted to the few stocked in most nurseries. If you do want a particular cultivar you will need to contact Brogdale or one of the specialist nurseries listed in *The Plant Finder*. This is an incredibly useful annual book which tells you exactly which nurseries stock which plants. Strictly speaking, the different quinces are cultivars, rather than varieties, but you may find them referred to as varieties by some nurseries and catalogues.

Much is often made of new cultivars which will ripen in Britain sufficiently so that one can eat the fruit straight from the tree. After an exceptionally long, hot summer this may be possible, but we rather feel this misses the point of quinces. You can eat apples, pears and many other fruits straight from the tree, quinces are the only fruits which will release such a wonderful flavour when cooked.

Below is a selection of the main cultivars available in Britain, with any particular characteristics or points of interest. Where it is not mentioned you can assume that the plant has smallish blossom and crops averagely well. The most widely available ones are described first.

Cydonia oblonga 'Vranja' Nenadovik (RHS Award of Garden Merit)

This is one of the most commonly found cultivars and is deservedly popular, being the only one with a coveted Award of Garden Merit. It originates from Vranje in south Serbia and was introduced into Britain in the 1920s. The buds are a stripey barber's pole pink and white and the blossom is sweetly scented. The fragrant pale green fruit ripens to a rich golden yellow. This will grow into a fairly upright tree, but can be fan trained if you start when the plant is young. It is the quince most resistant to blight.

C. o. 'Leskovac'

This is one of the hardiest cultivars and crops well, with large apple shaped fruits. On dwarfing rootstock it grows into a neat shape and is perfect for small gardens and growing in containers.

C. o. 'Lusitanica' syn. 'Portugal'

This cultivar was brought to England by John Tradescant in 1611, when it was described as the best quince for baking. This is a vigorous tree but can be slow to crop. It is not particularly hardy and needs to be grown in a sheltered spot. Given the right conditions it is an excellent choice, being very disease resistant, second only to 'Vranja'. The blossom is large and a beautiful pale rose colour. This is followed by largish (100 mm / 4 inches), fragrant, pear-shaped fruits. These turn a deep orangey-yellow and are covered with a thick woolly down. The flesh is tender and juicy and is still regarded by many as the best for all types of cooking. You need to provide a regular supply of water otherwise the fruit has a tendency to split.

C. o. 'Meech's Prolific'

This cultivar was raised in 1850 in America by the Rev. W. W. Meech. It fruited better that the already popular 'Orange', giving rise to its name; prolific. It has big flowers and large pear-shaped fruits which can reach 150 mm (6 inches) long. The fruits tend to ripen early and have an excellent flavour. The tree will also bear fruit early, often after only three years.

C. o. 'Agvambari'

C. o. 'Aromatnaya'

C. o. 'Bereczki'

This cultivar is Serbian in origin and is called after the Hungarian pomologist Bereczki. It is a very good cropper, with large fruits and is one of the best varieties for fan training.

C. o. 'Champion'

This nineteenth-century American cultivar is very productive, with large roundish fruits, which are mildly flavoured and ripen towards the end of the season. The blossom has pretty stripey buds which open into pale pink flowers. The tree will bear fruit when young, but is susceptible to blight.

C. o. 'Early Prolific'

C. o. 'Ekmek'

C. o. 'Iranian Quince'

This cultivar, fairly obviously, comes from Iran. The fruit is sweeter and less gritty than many of the other varieties and it keeps its shape well when cooked.

C. o. 'Isfahan'

This cultivar comes from Iran and is romantically named after the ancient city of Isfahan.

C. o. 'Ivan'

This is a recent introduction from Russia which ripens early. It is said to be possible to eat the fruit straight from the tree after a warm summer.

C. o. 'Krymsk'

Another recent cultivar from Russia, reputed to ripen fully in Britain after good summers.

C. o. 'Maliformis'

> This cultivar has apple shaped fruits with a fine flavour. It is very productive and the fruit ripens well in colder areas.

C. o. 'Pear-Shaped'

C. o. 'Rea's Mammoth'

C. o. 'Seibosa'

C. o. 'Serbian Gold'

C. o. 'Shams'

> The fruit on this cultivar from Iran is particularly sweet and less gritty than many others.

C. o. 'Smyrna'

C. o. 'Sobu'

> This is a large cultivar from Turkey which crops reliably; unfortunately the pear-shaped fruit can lack flavour.

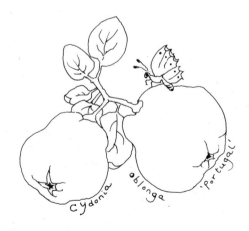

Many gardens that you can visit now grow quince trees either in orchards or as ornamental trees. Some have festivals in spring or autumn to celebrate the blossom and harvest respectively. The Orchard Network (www.orchardnetwork.org.uk) is a partnership of organisations working together for the conservation of traditional orchards as wildlife habitat. The website has lots of information about orchards to visit, nurseries selling fruit trees, news and events throughout the year. For quince enthusiasts, however, the following three sites should be top of the list.

The Walled Garden, Norton Priory
Tudor Road, Manor Park, Runcorn, Cheshire, WA7 1SX
Tel: 01928 569895
www.nortonpriory.org

This is the National Collection of Cydonia oblonga and has 24 different cultivars. It also has a good selection of Chaenomeles. The trees are in a charming 2½ acre walled garden attached to the ruins of a medieval priory. The garden is open daily apart from 24–26 December and early January. In October they host a Quince Day with guided tours. Dates for this vary, but it is usually on a Saturday towards the end of the month.

Royal Horticultural Society Garden, Wisley
Wisley, Surrey, GU33 6BQ
Tel: 0845 260900
www.rhs.org/Gardens/Wisley

Wisley has a delightful quince orchard with twelve cultivars. Some of the trees are quite young, whilst the older ones give you an idea of the lovely twisty shapes the trees can grow into. As all the varieties are planted together it is a brilliant place to compare them. The garden is open daily apart from Christmas Day. Times vary according to the seasons.

Brogdale Collections
Brogdale Farm, Brogdale Road, Faversham, Kent, ME13 8XZ
Tel: 01795 536250
www.brogdalecollecting.co.uk

Amongst the apples, pears and plums there is a large quince orchard, protected by high hedges. It is traditionally laid out and under-planted with wild flowers, including cowslips, kidney vetch, self heal, common trefoil, yellow nettle and crested dog's tail. Other quinces are planted in pairs throughout the main orchards and the collection has 19 different cultivars. It is open from late March to the end of October, with daily guided tours of the whole orchard.

QUINCES IN THE KITCHEN

Quinces usually need to be cooked before you can eat them, but they are extremely versatile fruits, suiting both sweet and savoury recipes. Raw quinces tend to be rock solid and sharp tasting, but cooking softens the flesh and, depending what you add, will change in colour to anything from the palest orangey pink to a deep, rich burgundy. The acidity is easily tempered and is actually an advantage in many dishes. It counteracts the greasiness found in fatty meats, in particular game, and quinces can be served in slices with the meat or as an accompanying sauce. In Britain quinces were traditionally served with partridge and in Germany and South Africa quince sauce is served with pork and mutton instead of apple or mint. The fruit complements middle-eastern tagines and stews and also go well with cheese, not just as the well known *membrillo*-manchego combination, but blue cheeses and the sharper goat's cheeses too.

In puddings they can be used to replace apples in almost any recipe, or in a combination with them. The addition of a little quince will bring a deliciously different taste to most apple or pear dishes. Equally, if you don't have enough quinces for a recipe you can always bulk them up with apples. The quince's sharpness means you can make wonderfully rich puddings with no danger of the sweetness becoming overpoweringly cloying. Afternoon tea brings to mind scones with quince jam or jelly, but quinces in cakes and biscuits are equally wonderful.

There is a surprising amount of juice in the fruits and drinks made from quinces range from delicious cordials and potent liqueurs. Finally, you can round off a meal with quince confectionery. They can be made into delicate, subtle chocolates or rich, gooey sweets.

Finally, a word of warning before you start cooking. Quince seeds are poisonous, containing tiny amounts of cyanide. You would need to eat an awful lot to actually do yourself any harm, but in most of the recipes they are removed at some stage. It is quite safe to cook the fruit with the seeds still in as long as you remove them at some stage.

BUYING

Between mid-October and the end of January quinces are fairly easily available in markets, greengrocers and, increasingly, supermarkets. Most of these fruits will be imported from the Mediterranean, Turkey and the Middle East and may be available up to March in some specialist delicatessens. Farmers' markets and greengrocers with local suppliers will stock British fruit, which is reputed to have a better flavour as it ripens on the tree for longer.

Specimens from abroad will be large and golden with a partial covering of fluffy grey down. Avoid any fruit with bruising or blemishes. Internal bruising is hard to spot, but does not really matter much as any slight discolouration will be hidden when you cook the fruit. South African quinces occasionally appear in early summer but these have travelled so far it is best to avoid them.

British quinces will look quite different. They are nearly always sold mixed, so you will be offered all shapes, sizes and even a range of colour from pale yellow to golden orange. The covering of down also varies according to the variety. A few blemishes on the skin don't matter and can be deceptive; the flesh can be fine even though the skin is marked. The appearance of home grown fruit can vary from year to year and it is always worth trying the fruit even if it doesn't look very prepossessing. The fruit won't have travelled far and with luck will only have been off the tree for a couple of days. Simply avoid anything that is shrivelled, squishy or obviously bruised. The skin should be firm and smooth and any softness will be a sign of damage rather than ripeness. Colour is the best indicator of ripeness. The fruit will progress from pale green to varying shades of yellow and gold, with the colour becoming richer and deeper as the fruit ripens. Less ripe fruit has the most pectin and is traditionally thought best for jams and jellies with the riper fruit being best for poaching and baking. In practice the overabundance of pectin in quinces means you can make preserves at any stage and they will always set.

PREPARING

Much is made of the awkwardness of having to cook quinces, but it is easy enough to gently simmer them and if you put them in the oven you don't even need to watch them. If you cut the quinces into thin slices you can use them in baked recipes without pre-cooking. The two puddings on pages 74 and 75 are examples of this. The disadvantages are that without slow cooking you don't get the wonderful pinky colours and the fruit doesn't have time to develop a depth of flavour. As they cook, there is the added advantage that the quinces will gently fill your house with their wonderful aroma.

Before they are cooked, quinces are rock hard. They are perfectly easy to peel, but coring can be difficult and even dangerous. Recipes which blithely say 'peel and remove the cores' seem to ignore how difficult coring can be. One method is to put the quince on a work-bench, place a piece of 18 mm internal diameter copper pipe over the top of the core and bash the pipe through with a hammer. (This is not recommended unless you are confident wielding a hammer; you cannot put the fruit in a vice as it will bruise.) If you cut the quince in very thin slices the core will fall away from each slice, but for this you need a sharp knife and a steady hand. Once baked or poached, the fruit is soft and it is simple to remove the cores which will pull away easily from the flesh.

STORING

Quinces will keep for at least a couple of months stored on trays in a cool, dark place as explained on page 29. Any longer than that and you either need to freeze or cook the fruit for reliable results. Fruit which you intend to use within a couple of weeks can simply be kept in a bowl. The varieties have different levels of fragrance and some will scent the room more strongly than others. There is no advantage to keeping the fresh fruits in the fridge.

You can freeze quinces whole. This is the easiest method and the fruit will keep for at least 6 months. Be very careful to choose perfect fruit and treat it gently so it does not bruise. Simply put the fruit into the deep freeze and then put into small, individual bags once frozen. Defrost the fruit at room temperature.

One of the best ways to freeze quinces is in blanched slices. They will keep for about 6 months and you can ensure you are only preserving good fruit. Peel and quarter the fruit. Bring a pan of water to the boil, add the quince slices and boil for two minutes. Drain and leave to cool. You can remove the cores now or leave them in to take out when the fruit is fully cooked. Store the fruit in small bags, each containing approximately one quince. These should be defrosted at room temperature and can be used in any of the recipes using sliced fruit or purée. You can cut the slices thinly and use them as they are or poach them in any of the liquids described on page 45.

You can also freeze quinces as a purée, either rough or smooth. This will keep for about 6 months and is useful to add to apple or pear dishes. For a rough purée peel the fruit and cut it into chunks, removing the core as you go. For every 450 g of chopped fruit add 2 tablespoons of caster sugar. Put the fruit and sugar into a heavy-bottomed saucepan and add enough water so the fruit is covered. Bring to the boil and simmer for 20–30 minutes until the fruit is just soft. Remove from the heat, allow to cool, and freeze in small plastic bags or rigid containers. Defrost at room temperature or add to pies straight from frozen. It is best to defrost the quince purée fully if you are adding it to other fruit so you can mix them together properly. At this stage you can also add sugar or lemon juice, as necessary.

For a smooth purée, peel the fruit but do not cut it up. Put it into a deep, heavy-bottomed saucepan and add sufficient water so the fruit is covered. Bring to the boil and then simmer until the fruit is soft. This will probably take between ¾ and 1½ hours. Remove from the heat, drain and allow the fruit to cool slightly. Pull the flesh away from the core and mash. If you want a really smooth purée you can put it through a mouli or sieve the pulp, but the latter is hard work and wastes a lot of fruit. Allow to cool and store in small plastic bags or rigid containers. As with rough purée this can be defrosted at room temperature or added directly to dishes which will be cooked.

THE RECIPES

It may be obvious to many readers, but just in case it's not; the quality of your ingredients really does make a difference. If you are going to invest time and effort in a recipe you might as well have the best raw materials you can get. Free range eggs taste better and the hens have a better quality of life. Outdoor reared meat has more flavour and vegetables grown without the addition of sprays and pesticides are better for you. Many of the recipes give you the option of making your own pastry or buying frozen. As long as you buy all-butter frozen pastry, it will be a perfectly good alternative.

In all the recipes, unless otherwise specified, butter is unsalted and eggs are large. Salt is coarse-grained and pepper is freshly-ground and black.

BAKED QUINCES

This is a good way to prepare the fruit, which can then be used in sweet or savoury dishes. The easiest way to bake quinces is simply to put them into the oven whole. To use this method you do need to know your fruit is in good condition as you cannot check it first. Wash all the furry down off. Heat the oven to 190°C/Gas 5 and cook until the fruit feels tender when gently squeezed. Depending on the size and ripeness of the fruit this will take between 1 and 2 hours. You want the fruit to remain reasonably firm, so stop before the flesh becomes squishy and begins to fall apart.

Once cooked, you can quarter the fruit and remove the core, or cut it in half lengthwise and scoop the core out. This is best done using a combination of a sharp, pointed knife and a melon baller.

Baked quinces were a favourite pudding of Sir Isaac Newton. You can serve them simply with a caramel sauce or stuffed with a variety of sweet or savoury fillings.

IDEAS FOR STUFFED QUINCES

Two suggestions for stuffed quinces are given on the following pages, but there are several simpler fillings or flavourings that can be added to the halved and cored fruit once it is baked. These might include:

Chopped nuts: walnuts, pistachios almonds or pine nuts
Honey
Cinnamon, vanilla or ginger
Dried fruit, especially raisins or sultanas
Brandy or any flavoured spirit
Freshly squeezed orange or lemon juice
Diced marzipan

Simply cut the cooked fruit in half, gently remove the core, pile on the filling and return to the oven for 10–15 minutes.

CORONATION QUINCES

At the coronation of Richard III in 1483 the last dish on the menu was 'Quynces Bake'. The instructions state that the quinces should be cored, filled with ginger and sugar and baked in a pastry coffin. Pastry coffins were commonly used in medieval cooking as a container for foods baked in an oven. They might then be decorated, but the were not necessarily eaten – the paste being coarse and dry. This modern variation omits the pastry and adds amaretti biscuits to the filling. They are certainly not authentic, but give the pudding a lovely crunchy topping.

Allow 1 medium sized quince per person.

For each quince

3 crunchy amaretti biscuits, crushed
1 tablespoon soft brown sugar
2 teaspoons amaretto liqueur
1 teaspoon powdered ginger

Preheat the oven to 190°C/Gas 5.

Bake the quinces whole as described above.

Mix the crushed biscuits, sugar, amaretto and ginger together in a bowl.

Remove the quinces from the oven and as soon as you can handle them, cut in half lengthwise. Remove the cores gently so as not to break the halves. Put back on the baking tray cut side up and pile the biscuit mixture on top of the quinces. Return to the oven for 15 minutes, until the topping has become crisp and caramel-flavoured, a truly wonderful combination.

Serve hot with lots of thick cream or ice-cream.

CAMEL DRIVER'S FEAST

Quinces grow wild in many parts of the Middle East and central Asia. Za'atar is a herb of the oregano family. The herb and spice mix to which it gives its name is the mainstay of many middle-eastern dishes. Here we have used equal quantities of sumac, dried thyme and sesame seeds, but you could perfectly well use a ready-made mix or a variation of your own.

Serves 2.

1 large quince (around 500g) or 2 medium ones
100 g couscous
olive oil
1 onion, finely chopped
200 g minced lamb
1 tablespoon barberries
2 tablespoons pine nuts
1 tablespoon za'atar (see note above)
salt & pepper

Preheat the oven to 190°C / Gas 5.

Bake the quinces whole as described above. Remove from oven and allow to cool. Cut in half lengthwise and remove cores carefully, try to avoid breaking the halves.

Measure out couscous and add twice the volume of boiling water (simply put the couscous into a jug and then add twice the amount of water.) Leave for 10–15 minutes to swell and soften. Add a tablespoon of olive oil, season with salt and pepper and fork through.

Fry the onion in oil until softened and translucent. Add the mince and brown off. If you have very fatty mince you may need to drain off any excess fat here. Add the barberries, pine nuts and za'atar and stir in. Season to taste. Place quinces in shallow baking dish. Pile the mince mixture into quince halves.

Mound the couscous over the mince. Drizzle with a little extra olive oil. Place in the oven and bake for 30 minutes.

Serve with salad and flatbreads.

POACHED QUINCES

Poaching brings out the full flavour of the fruit and gives it a lovely texture which is soft and yet firm. Depending on the poaching liquid you use, the colour will change to anything from a pale rosy pink to a deep mulberry purple. The slow cooking time needed may seem a hassle, but the quinces can simmer quietly on a back burner or sit in the oven at a low heat, gently softening and absorbing the flavours while you get on with other things.

You can poach quinces in any way from whole and unpeeled to cut into small chunks. Depending on the size of the fruit poaching them whole will probably take somewhere between ½ and 1½ hours. They are ready when you can easily insert the point of a knife into the fruit. They should be soft, yet firm enough to hold together; you do not want the flesh to disintegrate. Cooking them whole has the advantage that it makes it very easy to remove the core once the flesh is soft, but you can only do this with fruit that is not bruised or damaged in any way.

If you are making jam or jelly you only need to wash the skins and brush away the furry grey down. The skin will dissolve when you boil the jam and will be strained away for the jelly and cordial. For most other recipes it is best to peel the quinces as it makes it easier to test if the fruit is cooked and it also makes it easier for the fruit to absorb the flavours in the poaching liquid. Another important reason for peeling is so that you can check that the fruit is not bruised. Although they seem very hard quinces are surprisingly delicate and bruise very easily and may be damaged on the inside even if they look okay on the surface. A bit of discolouration doesn't matter as the fruit will change colour when you cook it. Just cut away any bits which are soft and brown as this is true bruising and will affect the taste.

The length of time you need to poach the quince for depends obviously on the size of the pieces and the hardness of the fruit and also on how much flavour you want it to absorb. The longer you poach it for the more it will take in and the deeper the colour will turn. As a very rough guideline the fruit needs 30 minutes to 1½ hours to cook and a good 2 hours to fully absorb the flavours and turn a rich ruby red. You can leave the fruit for as long as 8 hours, but for most recipes 2 hours will be ample.

BASIC POACHING METHOD

For most recipes using poached fruit in this book the easiest method is to peel, then quarter the fruit. As you cut the quarters into smaller slices you can easily remove the core as you go. This is much easier than trying to remove the core all in one go.

Quinces can be cooked in a variety of liquids from plain water to spicy red wine according to how you want to use them. The liquid should cover the fruit and simmer gently. Cover the pan with a tight-fitting lid and cook until the fruit is just soft. This can take anything from ½ to 2 hours, depending on the ripeness of the fruit. Start checking after about 30 minutes by inserting the point of a knife into the fruit, when it slides in easily the fruit is cooked. At the same time check that the liquid still covers the fruit. Once the fruit has cooked, you can gently remove it and boil the remaining liquid down to get a delicious, thick sauce. This can be stored in a lidded container in the fridge and will keep for a couple of weeks.

Plain water: This will give you pale-coloured fruit which can be used in mild-flavoured recipes.

Lemon: It is always worth adding a squirt of lemon juice to the water to prevent any cut or peeled fruit turning brown. Lemon juice is also handy to avoid the cloying sweetness you can get from boiling the fruit in syrup. A good starting point is the juice of half a small lemon for each quince. You can always add more at the end if the fruit isn't tart enough. Alternatively, you can add a couple of strips of lemon rind to the poaching syrup and adjust the sweetness at the end with juice.

Sugar syrup: If you poach quinces slowly in sugar syrup they will turn a fine pink colour. To get a really rich colour slow does mean slow and you need to simmer the fruit for a good 2 hours. The amount of sugar you use will depend on the individual dishes, but as a rough guide you need somewhere in-between equal amounts of sugar and fruit and half sugar to the weight of fruit. The sweetness can be tempered with the addition of lemon juice towards the end.

Honey: This is a good alternative sweetener to sugar. Always use light honey so it will dissolve easily and be absorbed into the fruit.

Red wine: This will give you a much deeper colour and is especially good if you want to create a spicy mix. Spicy quinces are particularly good with gently flavoured meat, such as chicken, and also make great puddings, served with vanilla ice-cream and plain biscuits. The herbs and spices which complement quinces are allspice, bay, cardamom seeds, chilli, cloves, cinnamon, coriander seeds, cumin, ginger, peppercorns, rosemary, star anise and vanilla (but obviously not all together). You can also add strips of orange or lemon rind. The recipes below will give you some ideas but they are really only a starting point.

Pomegranate juice: This will turn the quinces an incredible rich purple colour. Always taste the juice first to check how sweet it is, as you will need much less sugar, probably only an eighth the weight of the fruit. You may find you do not need to add any at all or that you need to add lemon juice to temper the sweetness.

Once poached the quince pieces should keep in the fridge for a couple of months. Keep in an airtight jar and ensure the fruit is submerged in the poaching liquid. Top up with water and a squirt of lemon if necessary.

SPICED POACHED QUINCES

This is totally delicious served on breakfast porridge with yoghurt. The rosewater version makes an excellent crumble. Just top with your usual crumble mix and put some slivered almonds on top. All three versions work well with ice-cream and shortbread. They can be used in any recipe where you want a mildly spiced flavour.

This mixture will give you beautiful rosy slices of fruit which are gently spiced and very versatile.

The quantities below will make about 3–4 jars

1 kg quinces (2 large or 3–4 medium)
170 g caster sugar
1 stick cinnamon
lemon juice

Spice options

Version 1: 4 whole cloves, 2 tablespoons rosewater

Version 2: 2 tonka beans (These are amazing and impart a gentle vanilla/almond/cinnamon flavour. You can get them from good spice shops or online)

Version 3: 2 whole cloves, 2 whole allspice berries, strip of orange or lemon peel (This version is best for savoury applications)

Fill a bowl with water and add a squeeze of lemon. Peel the quinces, keeping the skins. Cut the quinces into quarters or eighths, depending on their size and remove the cores. Put the slices into the lemony water straight away so they won't discolour.

Fill a large, heavy-bottomed saucepan with 2.4 litres water. Add the skins and cores to the water, bring to the boil, then cover and simmer gently for about 30 minutes. This is to extract the full flavour, and the pectin, which will make the final liquid deliciously syrupy.

Strain the skins and cores and return the liquid to the pan. Add the sugar, cinnamon stick and whichever spices you choose. Heat gently, stirring until the sugar dissolves. Add the fruit, cover and simmer for 1½ to 2 hours until the fruit is tender. Check every so often to make sure the quinces are submerged, adding more water if necessary. The fruit will gradually turn a vibrant pink. Remove the fruit and put in sterilized jars. It will be very soft and will break easily so be gentle. If making Version 1 add the rosewater to the syrup. Add the syrup to the jars, ensuring the fruit is covered.

This should be stored in a refrigerator and will keep for a couple of months.

OVEN-POACHED VANILLA QUINCES

This is a good basic poaching recipe. It will give you rosy pink fruit which is mild in flavour and can be used in almost any sweet dish. The cooking time is long, but providing the pan's lid fits snugly you can simply leave it and forget about it. Two added bonuses are that your house will smell amazing and you also get a delicious quince-flavoured syrup at the end.

6 medium quinces
2.25 litres sugar syrup; somewhere between 2 parts water to
    1 part caster sugar and 4 parts water to 1 part caster sugar,
    according to taste
juice of 1–2 lemons
1 vanilla pod, split

The amount of sugar and lemon you use will obviously determine how sweet the fruit is and the quantities are entirely up to you. A sugar syrup with a ratio of 2:1 water to sugar and the juice of 1 lemon will give you a very sweet, syrupy fruit whereas at the other extreme a sugar syrup of 4:1 and 2 lemons will give you fruit which is quite tart.

Preheat the oven to 150°C/Gas 2.

Put the water and sugar in a large pan and heat gently until the sugar has dissolved. Add the lemon juice and vanilla pod. Peel the quinces, then cut into quarters or sixths and remove the cores. Put the fruit straight into the syrup otherwise it will turn brown. Put the cores into a muslin bag and tie closed. This will thicken the syrup.

Put everything, including the muslin bag, into a dish with a tight-fitting lid and put into the oven. Leave for at least 2 hours. Do not stir. The quinces will turn a rich pinky red, the colour deepening the longer you bake them. Many recipes suggest up to 8 hours but if your fruit is at all ripe it will simply turn mushy. Two to two and a half hours should give you well-flavoured, nicely coloured fruit which is soft but still holds together. Gently pierce the fruit with the point of a knife after a couple of hours to see how it is doing and adjust the time accordingly.

Remove from the oven and leave to cool.

Remove the fruit and put in sterilized jars. It will be very soft and will break easily so be gentle. Add the syrup to the jars, ensuring the fruit is covered. This should be stored in a refrigerator and will keep for a couple of months.

Any spare syrup can be used as a cordial, for the pouring custard on page 77 or as a glaze for fruit tarts.

GINGER POACHED QUINCES

This gives you a much less sweet version than the previous recipe. The fruit goes well in salads, tagines and couscous. It can also be used to make the most amazing trifle.

The quantities below will make about 3–4 jars

1 kg quince
1 bottle ginger wine (Stone's or Crabbies for preference)
2 star anise
6 cloves
350 g runny honey

Put everything except the quinces in a saucepan.

Peel the quinces and cut into quarters or eighths depending on the size. Remove the cores and put into a muslin bag, this makes it easier to remove them later. Add the quince slices and muslin bag to the pan. If necessary top up with water so the fruit is covered.

Bring to the boil and then reduce heat to a simmer. Put a circle of baking paper over the liquid and put the lid on the pan. Simmer for 40–60 minutes. The fruit is ready when it yields to the point of a knife.

Gently remove the quinces and place in sterilized jars. Strain the cooking liquid, remove the muslin bag and pour the liquid over the quinces, ensuring the fruit is covered. Top up with water, if necessary. This should be stored in a refrigerator and will keep for a couple of months.

RECIPE IDEAS FOR POACHED QUINCES

Any of the above poaching liquids would work well here, although the trifle is particularly good with the ginger version.

COUSCOUS

Make the couscous according to the instructions on the packet, mixing in sultanas and dried apricots so they soak up the liquid. When it is ready, fluff up the couscous and add lemon juice to taste. Add pomegranate seeds and poached quinces, cut in chunks. Garnish with parsley.

SALADS

Poached quince slices are an excellent addition to many salads. They go particularly well with peppery salad leaves, radicchio, blue cheese, nuts and game. Good combinations are watercress, Stilton and walnuts or a variation of Waldorf salad with quinces, celery, mayonnaise and lemon juice on a bed of lettuce. Our favourite salad is one of bresaola and fennel. You simply toss shaved Florence or bulb fennel, shaved celery and courgette ribbons in a lemon juice vinaigrette. Line a dish with thin slices of bresaola, add the fennel salad and top with finely sliced poached quince.

AWESOME BUT EASY TRIFLE

You can make your own Madeira cake and custard, but if you use good quality bought versions this remains a spectacular dessert, with the added benefit of being almost instant. It looks best made in individual glasses. Dip the glass rims in melted white chocolate and then in pink sugar crystals. Cut the Madeira cake into cubes and moisten with the juices from some gingered quinces. Place the cake at the bottom of the glasses, add a layer of chopped poached quinces, a layer of custard and finally some slivered almonds and /or chopped crystallized ginger.

AN INDULGENT DRINK

Most left-over poaching liquid can be made into a drink by diluting with still or sparkling water. For a more indulgent version, add sparkling wine.

PRESERVES

GENERAL GUIDELINES FOR MAKING JAM AND JELLY

Making jam and jelly is perfectly simple and incredibly satisfying, but there are one or two points to be aware of. Unless specified, the instructions below apply to both jam and jelly even though we have referred only to jam.

The type of sugar you use will not alter the taste of the jam but it will affect how it sets. Most importantly you must always use cane sugar rather than beet. Apparently in chemical terms there is no difference between the two, but cane sugar sets much better. If you use beet sugar your preserve will take ages to make and will always be on the runny side. Whether you use granulated or preserving, refined or unrefined is entirely up to you. Preserving or jam sugar is more expensive than granulated and not quite so readily available. The individual grains of sugar are larger and this means they dissolve more easily and, in turn, this speeds up the whole process. It is good if, like us, you are impatient but it doesn't make better jam. Using refined or unrefined sugar is entirely a matter of personal preference.

The aspect of jam making which tends to worry people most is the setting point. This is the point at which the hot bubbling liquid in your pot will set when it cools. It is crucial not to overcook jam or jelly as they can become solid and rubbery and may taste burnt. The important thing to remember is that though you can always cook the jam a bit more, you cannot uncook it. With this in mind, always remove the pot from the heat when you test the jam. This way it will immediately stop cooking. It does not matter how many times you do this, you can even recook cold jam if you decide it is not sufficiently set. Testing whether the jam is set is very simple. Before you start put several saucers into the deep freeze. When you think the jam may be ready, remove it from the heat and, using a teaspoon put a small amount of jam onto one of the cold saucers. The jam will rapidly cool. Push your finger through it and if it forms a wrinkly skin it means the jam is ready and will set when cooled in jars. The jam is then ready to pour into jars. If it remains runny replace the pan on the heat and retest using another cold saucer.

When cooking the jam you will probably find a scum forms on the surface. Do not scoop this off while the jam is cooking as you will end up wasting a lot. When making jam you can disperse the scum by adding a little butter. Once the setting point has been reached, put a knob of soft butter into the jam and stir it until it melts. Any scum will miraculously disappear. The amount of butter you need will depend on the quantity of jam you are making and how much scum there is, so start with about ¼ teaspoon and add a little more if necessary. When making jelly you will need to scoop the scum off eventually as it will spoil the clarity of the jelly. Once the jelly has reached setting point allow it to cool slightly and then scoop off all the scum using a clean spoon. It doesn't look terribly attractive, but tastes just as good and can be put in a separate jar and eaten.

It is important to sterilize your jars properly otherwise you run the risk of the jam going mouldy. It is perfectly okay to remove any mould and eat the jam below but it doesn't look very good if you give away a jar of proudly made jam and a layer of blue mould has crept in. To sterilize, first preheat the oven to 110°C/Gas ¼. Wash the jars and lids thoroughly in hot, soapy water and rinse well. You can run them through a cycle of a dishwasher if you prefer. Put the jars upside down in the oven and leave them until they are totally dry. If you are using metal lids they can go in the oven too. Drying the jars in the oven removes the risk of wiping them with a less than spotless cloth and also means that they are hot and will not crack when you pour the hot jam into them.

When cooking, simmer the fruit slowly to break it up and dissolve the sugar. Then boil it rapidly, as the quicker it reaches the setting point the better the flavour will be.

Variously known as *membrillo, cotognata, cotignac*, quince cheese or quince paste, depending which country you are in, this is probably the best-known use for quinces. In Spain it is traditionally served with Manchego, a hard sheep's cheese and is so popular that the combination is called *Romeo e Julieta*. If you can't get Manchego it doesn't really matter as *membrillo* goes just as well with any sharp goat's cheese, mature Cheddar or even Stilton. If you live near a Spanish or middle-eastern delicatessen you will be able to buy *membrillo* cheaply. It is fast becoming more widespread but, be warned, it may be labelled as 'jelly' rather than cheese or paste. Like many things there are different qualities of *membrillo*, but none of the commercial products will compare with that which you make at home. This is because when you make your own you can adjust the sweetness and consistency so it is exactly as you like.

Making *membrillo* is slow but extremely easy as most of the time the fruit can be left to get on with it on its own. It is a very good way of using up fruit which is past its best because although you can't use badly bruised fruit it doesn't matter if the flesh is starting to turn brown. The level of pectin drops as fruit gets older, but quinces have so much to start with that you shouldn't have a problem with the *membrillo* setting regardless of how old your fruit is. The quantities here are very flexible, but as a rough guideline 3 largish quinces will give you a 150 mm, or six-inch, square of *membrillo* if you sieve the fruit, and a bit more if you use a food processor to make the pulp.

> *quinces*
> *granulated sugar*
> *lemon juice, to taste*

Line a 25 mm deep baking tray with greaseproof paper in readiness for the paste. Then, you need to cook the fruit so it is really soft.

The first method for cooking the fruit, and the easiest and best way (although the fruit itself should be in good condition without too many bruises) is to preheat the oven to 170°C / Gas 3, put the whole quinces on a tray lined with tinfoil and leave for two hours. This method also tends to give a more intense flavour as the fruit does not absorb any water.

Once the fruit is cooked remove it from the oven and leave to cool. Peel away the skin and remove the cores. Blitz the fruit in a processor so you have a nice smooth pulp, or push through a sieve.

An alternative method, if your fruit is really dodgy, is to remove the bad bits and then cut the remainder into chunks. Do not remove the skin or pips at this stage. Put the chunks into a heavy-bottomed saucepan and barely cover with water. Bring the water to the boil and then simmer until the fruit is soft. Depending on the fruit, this may take about an hour and during that time you need to keep an eye on it, adding a little water if necessary and stirring occasionally to ensure the fruit doesn't stick. When the fruit is really soft remove it from the heat and leave to cool.

Once the fruit has cooled cut away the cores and remove the skin. Blitz the flesh in a processor so you have a nice smooth pulp, or push through a sieve.

Whichever method you have chosen, you now have skin- and pip-free pulp which you can weigh. Add an equal amount of granulated sugar. Put both in a heavy-bottomed saucepan and heat gently until the sugar has dissolved. Bring to the boil and simmer until the mixture is very stiff and pulls away from the side of the pan. You will have to stir it regularly, but be careful as it will bubble and spit like a small volcano. Once it has achieved the correct consistency, taste and add lemon juice if necessary; a quarter of a lemon for 3 quinces should give a good flavour.

When the mixture is ready pour it into the tray and flatten it out so it is about 10 mm deep. Leave the tray uncovered in a warm place for about 12 hours so that it sets. An airing cupboard is ideal.

Wrap in clingfilm and store in an airtight container. It will keep almost indefinitely.

QUINCE JAM

This is a fine jam which is not too sweet and really thick with fruit. If you haven't made jam before, please read the notes on page 52. Making delicious jam is very easy, but there are one or two pitfalls that you need to avoid.

> *1 kg quinces*
> *1.5 kg granulated or preserving sugar*
> *juice of 2 lemons*
> *1800 ml water*

This will make between 3 and 6 jars depending how juicy the quinces are and how runny you like your jam.

Put a couple of saucers in the freezer to be ready for testing the jam.

Wash the jars and put in a low oven (110°C/Gas ¼) to dry.

Wash the quinces, removing all the fluff and cut out any bruised flesh. Put in a steel pan, cover the fruit with water and simmer until soft. This should take between half an hour and 1½ hours depending on the size of your quinces. Check periodically to ensure the pan does not dry out.

Lift the quinces out one at a time, place on a saucer, pull apart with a knife and fork and remove the core. You do not need to worry about the skin as this will break up when you boil the jam. The fruit will fall apart as you remove the cores. Cut the pieces into dice-sized chunks.

Return the quinces to the juice in the saucepan and add the sugar and lemon juice. Heat gently to dissolve the sugar and then boil hard until the setting point is reached. (See under general guidelines on page 52.)

Pour the jam into sterilized jars, seal and label when cool.

QUINCE JELLY

One of the joys of this jelly is the beautiful, clear colour, quite apart from the fabulous taste. It can be eaten on toast or scones and is also a delicious accompaniment to chicken, turkey and pheasant. If you haven't made jelly before, please read the notes on page 52.

1 kg quinces
sugar – granulated or preserving

Depending on the fruit 1 kg of fruit will give you about 300 ml of juice which will, in turn, make just over a jar of jelly.

Wash the quinces and rub off the fluffy down. Remove any bruised or blemished parts and cut all the rest into chunks, you don't need to worry about peeling or coring.

Put into a large, heavy-bottomed saucepan and add enough water so the fruit is just submerged.

Bring to the boil and simmer until the fruit has turned to pulp. Stir and squash down periodically to help the fruit break up and to prevent it sticking. This will probably take a couple of hours.

Pour the contents into a jelly bag and allow the juice to drip through into a bowl. It is easiest if you spoon the fruit into the bag first and then pour the liquid over. The whole operation is quite difficult and much simpler with two people, one to hold the bag open and one to pour. Do not squeeze the bag or press the fruit down as this will turn the jelly cloudy. The jelly will take a couple of hours to drip through and can be left overnight.

Put a couple of saucers in the deep freeze to use for testing the jelly.

Wash the jars and put in a low oven (110°C/Gas ¼) to dry.

Measure the juice and for every 500 ml juice add 400 g sugar. Put into a clean saucepan and heat gently until the sugar has dissolved. Once the liquid is clear, turn up the heat and boil hard until setting point is reached. (See under general guidelines on page 52.)

Pour into hot, sterilized jars, seal and once the jars are cool, label.

QUINCE CURD

This is a good alternative to the more usual lemon or orange curd. It eats well on bread or toast and makes a great filling for pies or tarts (see the chocolate tart on page 82). Out of season, you can make it using *membrillo* rather than fresh quinces.

Makes about 2 jars.

2 good, large quinces
granulated sugar
juice of ¼ lemon

or, if fresh fruit is not available, 500 g membrillo

75 g butter
2 eggs, lightly whisked

Preheat the oven to 170°C/Gas 3. Put the whole quinces on a baking tray lined with tinfoil and leave for 2 hours, by which time they should be soft. Baking the quinces this way means they do not absorb any water and will give the curd a really intense flavour.

Once the fruit is cooked, remove it from the oven, peel away the skin and remove the cores. Blitz the fruit in a processor so you have a nice smooth pulp, or push it through a sieve.

Weigh the pulp and add an equal amount of granulated sugar. Put both in a heavy-bottomed saucepan and heat gently until the sugar has dissolved. Bring to the boil and simmer until the mixture is very stiff and pulls away from the side of the pan. Be careful as it will spit. Add the lemon juice and mix.

Reduce the heat to a bare bubble, add the butter and whisk until it and the quinces are combined.

If you are using *membrillo*, soften it over heat and mix it with the butter.

The finished curd can be quite grainy. To get a smooth finish you now need to push the mixture through a sieve. This can be quite time-consuming as it is thick, but if you persevere most should go through, leaving the grainy strands of fruit behind.

Break the eggs into a separate pan and whisk. Put over a very low heat, add the quince mixture and whisk for about 5 minutes until everything is fully combined. At no point should the mixture come near boiling: you do not want scrambled eggs.

Remove from the heat, pour into warm, sterilized jars and seal.

This will keep in a refrigerator for a couple of months after it has been opened.

SPICED PRESERVED QUINCES

This is a brilliant way to store quinces as, if anything, the flavour improves with age. They can be added to lamb stews or tagines and go well with cheese or cold meat. You can eat them after a week, but are better for a longer storage.

The quantities below will fill 3 x 400 ml jars

1 kg quinces
500 ml cider or wine vinegar
750 ml water (the quinces need to be covered)
100 g light brown sugar
6 juniper berries; 8 whole peppercorns; 1 cinnamon stick
3 bird's-eye chillies (optional)

Peel the quinces and cut into quarters or eighths depending on the size. Remove the cores and discard.

Bring the vinegar and water slowly to the boil. Add the sugar and stir to dissolve. Add the quinces, juniper berries, peppercorns and cinnamon stick, turn down the heat and simmer for 30–45 minutes until the quinces are tender but still firm. Gently put the fruit into warm sterilized jars. Pour the poaching liquid over the quinces, ensuring that the fruit is covered.

If you are using the chilli, run a knife down the sides to split, but keep whole. Remove the seeds or not, depending on how hot you want your quinces, and put one in each jar. Seal well and put in a cool dark place for a month before using.

DUCK BREASTS WITH QUINCE SAUCE

Flavoursome quinces are the perfect accompaniment for rich and tender duck breasts, especially with the sweetness of the honey.

Serves 4.

4 duck breasts (boned but with the skin on)
1 tablespoon olive oil
salt and pepper
2 small lemons
600 ml water
3 medium quinces, peeled, quartered and poached in water and
  lemon (see the basic poaching method on page 45)
20 g butter
25 g fresh grated ginger root
30 ml clear honey
2 tablespoons sherry

Preheat the oven to 200°C/Gas 6.

Score the duck breasts, season well with salt and black pepper, drizzle olive oil over them and put in a tin with the skin side up. Roast for 30 minutes until the skin is crisp and golden. Allow to cool and cut the breasts into thin slices.

Cut the quince quarters into thin slivers, removing the core as you go. Melt the butter in a frying pan, add the quince slices and fry until brown. Remove the quince and place in a dish to keep warm.

Take 2–3 tablespoons of the duck fat and add to the frying pan, stirring in the ginger and honey for a minute before adding the remaining lemon juice and 3–4 tablespoons of water. Remove from the heat and finally add the sherry.

Arrange the duck breasts in a dish with the quinces and pour over the ginger sauce. Serve immediately with brown rice or couscous.

PORK FILLET WITH QUINCE AND CHESTNUT MUSHROOMS.

This is one of those simple recipes where the quality of the ingredients makes a real difference. If you can, it is best to use outdoor reared pork.

Serves 4.

500 g outdoor reared pork fillet

For the marinade
2 tablespoons olive oil
200 ml sherry
2 tablespoons clear honey
salt and pepper

2 medium quinces poached in water and lemon
    (see the basic poaching method on page 45)
25 g butter
olive oil
1 medium onion, finely sliced
125 g chestnut mushrooms, sliced
light soy sauce
2 cloves of garlic, chopped

Mix the marinade ingredients. Place the pork fillet in foil in a roasting tin and add the marinade. Leave for 3–4 hours.

Preheat the oven to 190°C / Gas 5.

Melt the butter in a frying pan and toss the quince slices until brown. Remove the quinces and set aside. Add a little olive oil to the frying pan and fry the onion, mushrooms and garlic, adding a splash of light soy sauce. Once the mixture is soft arrange it on top of the meat, then crown with the buttered quinces. Cook in the centre of the oven for 30–35 minutes; serve with mashed potatoes and fresh peas or green beans.

LAMB AND CHICKPEA TAGINE WITH COUSCOUS

This is a lovely middle-eastern stew, combining sweet and spicy flavours. The chickpeas give body to the stew and the couscous soaks up the juices beautifully.

Serves 4.

1 kg lamb shoulder (trimmed and cubed) or 4 lamb shanks
½ teaspoon cumin seeds
½ teaspoon coriander seeds
75 g butter
1 teaspoon ground ginger
½ teaspoon cayenne pepper
3 garlic cloves, crushed
2 onions, roughly chopped
400 ml water
250 g dried chickpeas, soaked overnight and rinsed
½ cinnamon stick
½ teaspoon ground cinnamon
4 tablespoons honey
1 large handful coriander, roughly chopped
salt and pepper
1 large quince, whole and peeled
2 strips lemon rind, cut lengthwise
½ teaspoon saffron threads, dissolved in a little water

couscous
olive oil

Preheat the oven to 150°C / Gas 2.

Grind the cumin and coriander seeds. Melt the butter in a casserole dish. Add the cumin, coriander, ginger and cayenne. Then add the garlic and onion. Coat well with the butter. Add the lamb, stir and mix everything well. Add 400 ml water, chickpeas, cinnamon stick, ground cinnamon, half the honey and a third of the coriander leaves. Bring to the boil, cover, put in the oven and cook for 1½ hours, or until the lamb is tender.

Put the quince in saucepan just covered with water. Add the remaining honey and the lemon rind and bring to the boil, before simmering and poaching until tender (half an hour to an hour depending on the quince's size). Save the poaching liquid.

When the lamb is cooked remove it and the chickpeas and keep them warm. Add about 3 tablespoons of the quince poaching liquid and the saffron to the meat juices. Reduce, taste and adjust the seasoning, if necessary.

Return the meat and chickpeas to the pan. Slice and core the quince and add to the pan. Cook the couscous according to the instructions, using half water and half quince poaching liquid. Fluff up the couscous with a fork, adding a splash of olive oil and season with salt and pepper to taste. Serve the lamb on a bed of couscous and scatter the remaining coriander leaves on the top.

PHEASANT WITH QUINCE

The beginning of the pheasant season coincides perfectly with the arrival of ripe quinces on the trees. The delicate meat goes perfectly with the quince gravy and caramelized slices of fruit.

Generally pheasants are not huge, one pheasant feeds two people comfortably with a bit left over and bones for stock, or you could stretch it to feed three if you serve plenty of vegetables.

1 quince
200 ml white wine
2 tablespoons honey
1 pheasant
small bunch thyme
2 rashers streaky bacon
1 generous tablespoon of quince jelly
425 ml pheasant or chicken stock
1 teaspoon caster sugar
15 g butter

Preheat oven to 220°C/Gas 7.

Peel and quarter the quince and remove the core. Put in a small saucepan with the wine and honey. Bring to the boil and then turn the heat down and simmer until the quince is cooked. This will take about 20 minutes; you want the fruit tender yet firm enough to hold together.

Season the pheasant well and place the thyme in the body cavity. Lay the bacon in a St Andrew's cross over the pheasant breast to prevent it drying out. Place the pheasant in a small roasting dish breast side uppermost. Put into the oven and roast for 15 minutes.

Turn the oven down to 180°C/Gas 4 and roast for a further 15 minutes or until the juices run clear when you pierce the thick part of the thigh joint. A little pink is not a bad thing with game; the cardinal sin is drying it out. Take the pheasant out and rest in a warm place, ideally breast side down.

If there is any excess fat in the roasting tin, spoon it out. Mix the quince jelly into the juices in the roasting pan and stir to melt the jelly. Add the stock and quince poaching liquid. Reduce till the gravy is syrupy.

Slice the quince. Melt the butter in a small frying pan, sprinkle over the sugar and cook the quince on both sides till slightly caramelized.

Stir any juices which have come out of the rested pheasant into the gravy and serve with the pheasant and caramelized slices of fruit.

MARINATED CHICKEN WITH BUTTERED QUINCE AND BLACK-EYED BEANS

You need to prepare the ingredients for this recipe the day before, but the actual cooking is quick and easy. In some southern states of America, black-eyed beans eaten on New Year's Day are thought to bring prosperity in the coming year.

Serves 2.

2 skinless, boneless chicken breasts

2 tablespoons of olive oil

black-eyed beans, either dried (which will need soaking
  overnight and boiling) or tinned

12 large slices of firm poached quince (use the basic poaching
  recipe with water and lemon on page 45)

40 g butter

a handful of small button mushrooms

50 g almond flakes

Marinade:

4 tablespoons runny honey

25 mm piece of fresh ginger root, peeled and finely grated

2 tablespoons orange juice

a generous squirt of garlic paste

2 tablespoons light soy sauce

salt and pepper

Make deep diagonal cuts into the top of each breast, taking care not to cut right through. Place the chicken breasts in an ovenproof dish with the oil in the bottom. Combine all the marinade ingredients in a bowl by whisking them together and pour over the meat, turning so it is well coated. Cover with clingfilm and leave in the fridge overnight.

If using dried beans soak them overnight and then boil in salted water for 30–40 minutes till soft, but not falling apart.

Preheat the oven to 220°C/Gas 7.

Remove the clingfilm and baste the chicken with the juice. Bake on a high shelf in the oven for 20–30 minutes.

While the chicken is cooking, gently fry the quince slices in the butter till golden brown. Add the mushrooms and fry for a further 5 minutes. Take the chicken out of the oven and carefully nestle the quince slices in and around the chicken breasts. Add the beans and mushrooms and scatter the almonds over the top. Return to the oven for a further 10 minutes.

Serve immediately with mashed potato and green vegetables of your choice.

QUINCE AND GOAT'S CHEESE TART

This is a fruit, cheese and nut course all in one. The subtle taste of lemon from the poached quinces filters through the rest of the ingredients and complements the cheese. This pastry is truly nutty, which adds a slightly crunchy dimension to the dish and can be used in many other tart or quiche dishes.

Pastry
50 g walnuts, finely chopped
150 g self-raising flour
1 tablespoon golden caster sugar
a pinch of salt
100 g cold unsalted butter
2 tablespoons cold water

Filling
150 g quince, peeled, cored and sliced (use basic poaching method on page 45 with water and lemon)
250 g soft goat's cheese
2 medium eggs
200 ml crème fraîche
110 ml double cream

Mix the walnuts, flour, sugar and salt together. Add the butter, chopping with a knife until the mixture resembles breadcrumbs. Gradually add the water to make a firm dough. Wrap in clingfilm and chill in the fridge for 30 minutes.

Preheat the oven to 200°C / Gas 6. Roll the pastry lightly on a floured board and then press into a greased 230 mm quiche tin. Blind bake the pastry for 20 minutes until a light golden colour. Leave it to cool and reduce the oven temperature to 190°C / Gas 5.

Scatter the chopped quince evenly over the pastry crust. Mix together the remaining filling ingredients and pour over the fruit.

Bake for 20–25 minutes until firm, and golden brown patches start to appear on the surface. Serve warm with salad. For a more substantial meal this is tasty with couscous.

HOT LIGHTNING

This charmingly named Dutch dish has many variations; this is based on one from the equally delightfully named book *Roast Figs and Sugar Snow* by Diana Henry. It is an excellent winter accompaniment to sausages or any pork cuts, especially roast joints.

Serves 6, generously.

1 kg small waxy potatoes (you can leave the skins on as it gives an attractive rustic look)
1 sharp eating apple, cored but not peeled
1 large quince, peeled, cored, cut into chunks and poached (use the basic poaching method on page 45 and remove the fruit when it is still quite firm)
50 g butter
salt, pepper, soft light brown sugar, to taste

Preheat the oven to 170°C/Gas 3.

Cut the potatoes into half, or small chunks.

Cut the apple and quince into chunks the same size as the potatoes.

Melt the butter in a heavy-bottomed pan and sauter the potatoes.

Add the fruit and mix well so it is all coated with the butter.

Season and add sugar to taste.

Put into a lidded casserole, add a little water and cook for about 45 minutes.

Stir everything around a couple of times to stop it sticking and add a little more water if necessary. The potatoes should be just soft. Serve immediately.

SPANISH PORK CHOPS WITH QUINCE SAUCE

This quince sauce is a lovely tart alternative to apples. Combined with the sherry and smoked paprika, this makes a fine Spanish feast.

4 pork chops
salt and pepper
olive oil
1 tablespoon smoked paprika
1 tablespoon fresh thyme (leaves stripped from the stalks)
2 tablespoons sherry (for real luxury make this Pedro Ximenez)

Sauce
500 g quinces
4 tablespoons water
3–4 tablespoons butter, soft
2 teaspoons sugar
squeeze of lemon juice

To make the sauce, peel the quinces and slice thinly, removing the cores as you go. If you cut the peeled quinces in half and then cut slices from the outside towards the core, you will find the fruit breaks off easily where the core starts. Put the slices straight into a small saucepan with the water, to stop them turning brown.

Place over a medium heat, cover and cook for about 20 minutes or until tender. Stir now and again to stop the quinces sticking. Remove from the heat and mash, either by hand or using a stick-blender.

Add the butter and stir until smooth. Add the sugar and a squeeze of lemon. Taste and add a little more sugar or lemon, if desired. This will keep in a jar in the fridge for about 4 weeks

Season pork chops with salt and pepper. Drizzle with olive oil and rub with smoked paprika and thyme leaves. Cover and marinate in the fridge for at least 30 minutes. If you do this in the morning, the chops will be perfect by the evening.

Heat a griddle pan or heavy-bottomed frying pan until hot.

Put the chops in the pan and cook until browned on both sides. The fat should be crisp.

Transfer the chops to a warmed serving dish.

Add the sherry to the pan and deglaze over a medium heat. You won't need to season as the flavours from the chops will mix with the sherry.

Drizzle the juices over the chops and serve with the quince sauce on the side.

SAVOURY QUINCE CAKES

This recipe is a meat alternative to a fish cake, using the same method of binding with egg and a little mashed potato, and coating them with beaten egg and breadcrumbs before frying. The addition of the quince provides a perfect contrast to the pork. They are best served with the remaining mashed potato and fresh vegetables. They can also be cooked on a barbecue; brush both sides with oil put on a wire rack.

Serves 4.

150 g poached quince, cubed (use the basic poaching method
  on page 45)
plain flour
600 g coarsely minced free-range or organic minced pork
150 g white button mushrooms, chopped
1 clove garlic, crushed
1 small white onion, finely cut
1 teaspoon ground cumin
2 teaspoons cumin seeds
2 teaspoons salt
1 teaspoon freshly ground black pepper
1 kg of creamy mashed potato (using 150 g of this for the burgers)

1 large egg, beaten
150 g coarse granary soft breadcrumbs
2 tablespoons vegetable oil

Toss the quince cubes in a little plain flour, in a large bowl and then add the pork, mushrooms, garlic, onion, spices and seasoning. Mix gently. Then add 150 g of the mashed potato and mix again. Put in the fridge to cool for 20–30 minutes.

Break the egg into a low shallow bowl (a large soup dish is ideal) and beat well.

Put the breadcrumbs into another similar bowl.

Warm the oil in large frying pan over a medium to high heat.

Take the meat mixture out of the fridge and make a small test patty using a couple of teaspoons of the mixture. Fry the patty for a couple of minutes on each side until thoroughly cooked and then taste. Make any adjustments to the seasoning, if necessary.

Shape the rest of the mixture into 8–9 medium-sized patties.

Take each patty in turn, firstly swiftly dipping into the egg, covering both sides and then generously coating it with the breadcrumbs.

Fry them gently in batches for 4–5 minutes on each side, so that they are a deep golden colour all over, but without burning them. They are quite delicate so take care when turning them. Keep them warm in a low oven until all the patties are cooked.

Reheat the rest of the mashed potato and serve with peas or beans.

SWEET DISHES

STAINED GLASS WINDOW TART

This is a really beautiful tart with the jam and jelly divided into patterns between pastry strips. You can make your own jam and jelly or buy them but make sure the jam is dark and fruity so you get a good contrast of colours. Serve hot or cold, with cream or ice-cream.

Serves 4 to 6.

quince jam, about ⅓ jar, depending how deep you want the tart
quince jelly, as above
shortcrust pastry (you can use ready-made, all-butter pastry or
*   make your own following the recipe on page 101, depending*
*   on your time and inclination)*
1 egg, beaten

Preheat the oven to 200°C/Gas 6.

Grease a 230 mm loose-bottomed tart tin. Set aside about one-third of the dough and, on a lightly floured surface, roll the rest out to line the base and edge of the tin. Tidy the edges.

Roll out the remaining dough and cut into thin strips. Dampen the edges and stick the strips down so they divide the tart into sections. A pinwheel pattern works well, as do concentric rings or a lattice-work. The important thing is to make sure that the strips are firmly fixed to the base as you do not want the jam and jelly to mix. The divisions must also be tall enough so the two won't bubble up and mix while cooking. Ideally they should be the same height as the edge of the tart.

Spoon the jam and jelly into alternate gaps and brush the pastry with beaten egg. This will give the pastry a glossy finish.

Bake for 25–30 minutes, until the pastry is crisp and a rich golden colour. Serve hot or cold, with cream, ice-cream or the quince custard on page 77.

GOLDEN QUINCE TART

This is a variation of traditional treacle tart, with *membrillo* in the syrup mixture and slices of poached quince on the top. Originally 'golden syrup' was known as 'pale treacle', giving rise to the fact that 'treacle tart' is actually made with 'syrup'. This tart is very pretty with the slices of fruit arranged on the top and is less cloyingly sweet than treacle tart can sometimes be. It is delicious hot and equally good cold, if you have any left.

Serves 4 to 6.

shortcrust pastry (you can use ready-made, all-butter pastry or
    make your own following the recipe on page 101, depending
    on your time and inclination)
250 g golden syrup
200 g membrillo
2 tablespoons cream
150 g breadcrumbs
juice of ½ lemon
2 quinces sliced and poached in water and lemon (use the
    basic poaching method on page 45 or the oven-poached
    recipe on page 48; the exact amount will depend on the
    size of the quinces; you need enough slices to spread on top
    of the tart, but how tightly you pack them is up to you)
quince syrup or jelly, to glaze

Grease a 230 mm loose-bottomed tart tin. On a lightly floured surface roll out the pastry so it lines the base and sides of the tin. Tidy the edges and prick the base with a fork. Return to the fridge for another ½ hour.

Preheat the oven to 200°C / Gas 6. Line the pastry case with greaseproof paper and fill with baking beans. Bake for 15 minutes, remove the beans and paper, reduce the temperature to 180°C / Gas 4 and bake for another 5–10 minutes to dry the pastry.

Put the golden syrup and *membrillo* in a saucepan and heat gently, whisking until they are mixed together. Remove from the heat.

Add the breadcrumbs and cream and whisk into the syrup

mixture. Add the lemon juice a little at a time, tasting to check how much you need.

Pour the mixture into the pastry case and arrange the quince slices on top. You can either put a layer of thin slices right over the tart, or arrange thicker slices in a pattern. Thicker slices, say 10 mm or half an inch, will give you contrasting textures between the fruit and the syrup mixture. Cover the fruit with a glaze, either reduced poaching syrup or gently heated jelly.

Bake for 40 minutes until set.

Serve hot or cold with cream or the quince custard on page 77.

ICE-CREAM

The wonderful thing about this ice-cream is that has an unctuous texture even without an ice-cream maker. It is very easy to make and, as it uses *membrillo* rather than fresh quinces, you can make it all year round.

Serves 4 to 6.

250 g membrillo
2 tablespoons lemon juice
1 tablespoon water
*1 tablespoon Madeira or quince liqueur (if you don't have these,
any apple-based liqueur will work just as well)*
300 ml double cream

Put the *membrillo*, lemon juice, water and alcohol in a pan and melt gently over a low heat. Stir well to combine all the ingredients. Allow to cool slightly.

Whisk the cream until it holds softly, but is not stiff. Fold the cream into the *membrillo* mixture, pour into a container and freeze. Leave for 4 hours or overnight. This ice-cream remains soft and can be served straight from the freezer.

SALLY'S CHARLOTTE

This recipe was given to us by Sally Hughes and has been passed down through her family. There are many variations of charlottes, but most are thought to be named after Queen Charlotte, the wife of George III. If you don't have enough quince you can add cooking apples to bulk it up.

Serves 4.

1.5 kg quinces
juice of 1 lemon
3–4 tablespoons caster sugar
4 thickish slices of good white bread
50 g butter

Preheat the oven to 190°C/Gas 5.

Peel the quinces and cut into slices removing the core as you go. This is easiest if you halve the peeled quinces and then cut the slices in towards the core. They will automatically break off where the hard core starts. Put the slices in a bowl of cold water with a squirt of lemon to stop them browning.

Drain the quinces and put in a saucepan with the rest of the lemon juice and sufficient water to just cover the fruit. Bring to the boil and then simmer for about 10 minutes. If you are using apple as well, peel, core, cut into chunks and add to the quince. Cook for another 10 minutes or until the fruit is soft enough to squash easily.

Put the fruit into a shallow baking dish. Taste and sprinkle 2–3 tablespoons sugar over the top, as necessary. Remove the crusts from the bread and cut each slice into two or four triangles, depending on the size. Spread each slice with butter and place in a single layer on top of the fruit. Sprinkle the remaining spoonful of sugar over the top and bake for 25 minutes or until the top has turned golden brown and crispy.

Serve hot with lots of thick cream.

SURPRISE PUDDING

This sponge is more of a pudding than an afternoon cake and is best served hot with a generous helping of custard or cream. Bake it in an attractive dish or tin so you can take it straight to the table. The syrupy quince layer is a delightful surprise beneath the crispy top.

3 or 4 medium quinces
6 tablespoons golden syrup
170 g butter
170 g self-raising flour
170 g soft brown sugar
3 eggs
85 g pecan nuts, halved lengthwise

Preheat the oven to 180°C / Gas 4.

Peel and core the quinces and cut into thin slices. This is easiest if you halve the peeled quinces and then cut the slices in towards the core. They will automatically break off where the hard core starts.

Spread the syrup in the bottom of a 230 mm non-stick round cake tin (not loose-bottomed) or pie dish and layer the quince slices on top.

Put the butter, flour, sugar and eggs in a food processor and mix. Add the pecans and spread the mixture over the quinces.

Bake for an hour, or until a skewer inserted in the middle comes out clean. Check after about 40 minutes and, if the cake is turning too brown, cover it with foil.

Serve with cream, crème fraîche, ice-cream or the quince custard on page 77.

SPICED QUINCE UPSIDE-DOWN PUDDING

This is a fabulous dark, rich, gooey cake which needs to be served hot with lots of cream, crème fraîche or ice-cream. We found it in the *National Trust Magazine* in autumn 1998 and have been cooking it ever since.

Cake mixture
180 g plain flour
1 teaspoon bicarbonate of soda
a pinch of salt
1 teaspoon ground cinnamon
90 g butter
120 g soft brown sugar
120 g black treacle
150 ml milk
1 egg, beaten

Topping
60 g butter
120 g soft brown sugar
3 or 4 medium-sized quinces
60 g sultanas (optional)
icing sugar, to decorate

Preheat the oven to 180°C/Gas 4. Grease a 200 mm cake tin.

Cream the butter and sugar for the topping together and spread across the bottom of the cake tin.

Peel and core the quinces and cut into thin slices. This is easiest if you halve the peeled quinces and then cut the slices in towards the core. They will automatically break off where the hard core starts.

Arrange the quince slices on the butter mixture in one or two layers and, if you are using them, sprinkle the sultanas on top.

For the cake mixture, sieve together the flour, bicarbonate of soda, salt and cinnamon into a bowl. Meanwhile, in a saucepan, gently heat the butter, sugar and treacle until well combined. Remove from the heat and allow to cool slightly. This ensures you will not end up with scrambled egg in the mixture. Beat in the egg and then the milk.

Beat the treacle mixture into the dry ingredients and pour over the quinces.

Bake for an hour or until an inserted skewer comes out clean. Test after about 40 minutes and if the top is browning too fast put a piece of tinfoil over it.

Turn out onto a serving plate and sprinkle with icing sugar. Serve hot with cream, ice-cream or the quince custard below.

POURING CUSTARD

This is based on a recipe from Eliza Acton's *Modern Cookery for Private Families*, which was written in 1845. It is thick and can be thinned with cream or left to cool totally in the fridge when it will set almost like a blancmange.

The quantities below will make a small jug of thick custard.

200 ml poaching syrup
4 egg yolks, beaten
single cream (optional, for a thinner custard)

The syrup left over from poaching quinces in the oven (page 48) is perfect for this custard, as it has a really strong quince flavour and also turns the custard a beautiful pink-orange colour.

Put the syrup into a small saucepan and heat until it begins to simmer. Pour it onto the egg yolks and mix well.

Pour this mixture into a clean saucepan and cook gently, stirring all the time, until the custard thickens (never allowing it to boil).

Strain into a bowl and leave to cool, stirring occasionally.

When the custard is cold, it can be thinned by stirring in single cream.

QUINCE AND APPLE PANCAKES

Pancakes are very quick and easy to make and extremely versatile; they can be either savoury or sweet. The fruit filling can be swapped with other combinations too. Remember any left-over batter always keeps fine in the fridge for a day or two. They are best served straight out of the pan, when everyone is seated, but can also be kept warm in a cool oven.

Pancake batter
125 g plain flour
a pinch of salt
1 egg, beaten
300 ml semi-skimmed milk
50 g chilled butter for shallow frying

Filling
250 g cooking apples, peeled, cored and sliced (put the slices in bowl of water with a little lemon juice to stop them turning brown)
25 g salted butter
250 g quince slices (use the basic poaching method on page 45 or the oven-poached recipe on page 48)
50 g demerara sugar
3 tablespoons lemon juice
2 tablespoons clear honey

Glaze to finish
3 tablespoons apricot jam, warmed with 1 tablespoon of boiling water

To make the pancakes, sift the flour and salt into a bowl. Add the egg and half the milk. Beat until smooth. To finish gradually beat in the remaining milk. Put into the fridge for an hour to chill.

Place the butter for frying into the freezer 10–15 minutes before starting to make the pancakes. The heat of the pan together with the cold butter creates the best pancakes.

Preheat the oven to 170°C/Gas 3.

Lightly grease a small (180 mm) frying pan by melting the chilled butter straight from the freezer, over a high heat. Remove the batter from the fridge and, if it feels a little stiff, stir in an extra dash of milk. When the butter is sizzling (be careful not to let it burn), pour in just enough batter to cover the bottom of the pan. Cook the pancake until it is golden brown underneath, then flip it and cook the other side. Put the pancake on a plate and place in the oven to keep warm.

Use the remaining batter to make 9–10 pancakes, stacking them, interleaved with greaseproof paper. You can also briefly place them onto some kitchen paper to absorb any excess fat, if time allows.

To make the filling, parboil the apple slices until slightly soft, for approximately 5–7 minutes.

Melt the butter in the frying pan and heat until sizzling. Add the apples, quinces, sugar, lemon juice and honey, stirring gently to prevent them sticking.

Turn the oven up to 180°C/Gas 4

Place a pancake on a greased ovenproof dish, cover with some of the quince and apple mixture, then place another pancake on top to make a pancake sandwich. Spoon over the apricot jam to glaze. Bake for 10–15 minutes until heated through.

Cut into wedges and serve immediately. These pancakes are fabulous served with natural yoghurt, which cuts through the richness. Runny honey is also a good addition.

TARTE TATIN

Tarte Tatin is a French upside-down apple tart and is called after the Tatin sisters who had a restaurant at Lamotte-Beuvron, south of Orleans. The story goes that Stéphanie, one of the sisters, was distracted while cooking apples in sugar and butter for a pie filling. The sugar caramelized and, rather than wasting the fruit, she covered it with a layer of pastry and baked it. When the dish came out it was inverted onto a plate and became an immediate favourite in the restaurant.

This pudding will convert any sceptics to the merits of quinces. You can use any poached quinces but the ginger cuts through any cloying sweetness in the syrup.

Serves 6.

500 g ginger poached quinces (page 49), ideally fairly firm (the amount of fruit is very flexible; you can always pad it out with alternate slices of apple if you don't have enough quince – use firm dessert apples such as Russets or Granny Smiths)

30 g light brown sugar

25 g butter

puff pastry (for us, the joy of this pudding is that it is very quick and easy to make so we use ready-made pastry. If you buy all-butter pastry it is a perfectly good alternative to home-made)

If you don't have a tatin pan, you can use a cast-iron frying pan or any similar dish. The crucial thing is that it must be able to go on the direct heat of the hob as well as in the oven. The amounts here are for a 240 mm tatin dish, but this is a very flexible recipe; a little either way won't matter.

Preheat the oven to 350°C/Gas 5.

Put the butter and sugar in the pan and heat gently, stirring, until the sugar has dissolved. Remove from the heat.

Peel, core and slice the apples, if using. The slices of quince and apple should be the same size. Cover the base of the pan with a layer of quince slices. Lay them close together and neatly as the dish will be inverted so the bottom will become the top. If you lay the slices in concentric rings, working from the edge of the dish in towards the middle the tart will look pretty and cook evenly.

Roll the pastry out on a floured work surface and cut a circle slightly larger than the pan. Place it over the fruit and tuck it over the quinces round the edge. Pierce with a sharp knife to allow any trapped air to escape.

Bake for 30–40 minutes until pastry is cooked and nicely browned.

Allow to cool slightly and turn the tart out carefully onto a flat dish. This sounds easy and looks impossible, but it actually perfectly simple. Do it while the dish is still fairly hot to prevent the caramel hardening. Run a sharp knife round the edge of the dish to make sure nothing has stuck. The easiest way to do this is to put the serving plate over the top of the pan, grasp the plate and dish firmly on either side and turn over quickly. It is easier to do this with a towel, rather than oven gloves, as they can be unwieldy. Rearrange any stray slices of fruit, if necessary.

The tart can be served hot, warm or at room temperature, but needs the addition of cream, ice-cream or crème fraîche.

QUINCE CURD AND CHOCOLATE TART

This recipe is a delicious combination of dark chocolate pastry and rich curd filling. You can either spread the cream in a layer on top of the curd, or serve in a separate bowl.

Serves 4–6.

Pastry
175 g plain flour
35 g icing sugar
50 g cocoa powder
100 g cold butter, cut into small chunks
1 egg yolk
2 tablespoons cold water
60 g plain chocolate

about half a jar of quince curd (the amount is flexible, as it is entirely up to you how thick a layer you want in the tart; see recipe on page 58)
300 ml double cream

First make the chocolate pastry. Sift the flour, icing sugar and cocoa together. Add the butter and either blitz briefly in a food processor or rub in with your fingertips. The mixture should be combined and resemble fine breadcrumbs.

Transfer to a bowl, make a well in the centre of the mixture and add the egg yolk. Mix in with one hand, adding the water a little at a time. Be careful not to add too much water, the mixture should just stick together to form a dough. Gently knead and form it into a ball. Wrap the dough in clingfilm and put in the fridge for 30 minutes.

Preheat the oven to 200°C / Gas 6. Grease a 230 mm loose-bottomed tart tin.

On a lightly floured surface, roll out the pastry so it lines the base and sides of the tin. Don't worry about tidying the edges too much; the tart looks better if they are left slightly rough. Prick the base with a fork. Line the pastry case with baking parchment and fill with baking beans. Bake for 10 minutes, remove the beans and paper, reduce the temperature to 180°C/Gas 4 and bake for another 10 minutes to dry the pastry.

Grate the chocolate, using a peeler rather than a grater; this will give you slightly larger shavings.

As soon as you remove the pastry from the oven, sprinkle half the chocolate shavings over the base of the tart. They will melt into the pastry and intensify the chocolate flavour. Leave the pastry to cool.

Whip the cream until firm. Spread a layer of quince curd over the base of the tart and then add a layer of cream (if adding to the tart). How thick you make these layers is up to you, 10–15 mm each should give a good balance of flavours and still allow the chocolate pastry edges to rise above the filling. Sprinkle the remaining chocolate over the top. Serve at room temperature.

QUINCE POTS

This is based on an eighteenth-century recipe from Hannah Glasse's *The Art of Modern Cookery Made Plain and Easy* (1747). These dainty puddings are deceptive; they are very rich and best in small quantities.

Serves 6 (or 4 if your guests are greedy).

150–225 g stiff quince purée (if it is very soft the custard will be too sloppy)
300 ml cream (single, double or mixed)
2 egg yolks
50 g caster sugar

First make the purée. Wash the furry down off the quinces and put them in a deep saucepan. Fill it with water so the fruit is submerged. Bring to the boil, cover and cook until the fruit is soft. Cooking the fruit whole takes longer than if you cut it up, but this way it absorbs less water and you want the paste as stiff as possible. One 500 g quince will take about an hour and a quarter and give you 300 ml of stiffish purée.

Remove the fruit, cut into chunks, remove the cores and put in a blender (or use a stick blender) to make the purée. Any left-over purée keep well in the freezer.

Preheat the oven to 170°C/Gas 3.

Beat egg yolks with sugar until pale and thick. Beat in the cream. Fold in the quince purée a little at a time, tasting as you add, until you have the flavour and consistency you want. Butter a baking dish or individual ramekins and pour in the mixture. Put into a bain-marie and bake till set. This will depend on the size of the dish or ramekins. Ramekins will give you elegant little desserts and will take 45 minutes.

A possible variation is to let the cooked custards cool, then scatter caster sugar over the top before caramelizing the tops under a grill, in the fashion of crème brûlée.

You can also flavour the quince purée with a tablespoonful of powdered ginger, or introduce the ginger by chopping a couple of knobs of candied stem ginger and folding them into the custard.

QUINCE AND APPLE SHORTCAKE

This recipe comes from Jan Greenland and first appeared in *Herbs* magazine. It is incredibly versatile as you can use almost any combination of different fruits; rhubarb and strawberries are a particularly good combination. Part of the shortcake is grated, creating a deliciously crunchy topping.

> *1 or 2 quinces and Bramley apples to make 450 g prepared fruit*
> *(use water and lemon and the basic poaching method on*
> *page 45)*
> *110 g soft butter*
> *65 g caster sugar*
> *1 small egg, beaten*
> *225 g self-raising flour*
> *2 tablespoons light oil*
> *a pinch of salt*

Peel, core and slice the fruit and then poach to make a purée. Stir 1 tablespoonful of the caster sugar into the quince and apple mixture and leave to cool.

Preheat the oven to 180°C/Gas 4.

Cream the butter and the rest of the sugar together. Add the beaten egg, a little at a time. Fold in the flour, oil and salt. Cut the dough in half, wrap one half in clingfilm and put it in the freezer for 30 minutes. Press the other half into a greased, loose-bottomed tin or ovenproof dish measuring 180 x 280 mm or 7 x 11 inches.

Spoon the fruit over the base.

Grate the rest of the chilled dough on the largest holes of a grater over the top, dipping it in flour if it becomes sticky.

Bake for 30 minutes until golden. Dust with icing sugar and serve warm or cold.

GINGER AND QUINCE CAKE

This is another recipe which is part afternoon tea, part pudding. Serve it warm with custard or put it on a pretty plate and serve it with a pot of tea and scones. In the unlikely event of any being left over, it stores well in an airtight tin.

225 g soft butter
125 g light brown sugar
100 g caster sugar
4 medium eggs
225 g self-raising flour
2 teaspoons baking powder
2 small pieces of stem ginger, diced
200 g firmly poached quince, diced (use the basic poaching method with water and lemon on page 45 and remove from the heat when the quince is still firm)
100 g walnuts and/or pecans (we like half and half)
demerara sugar, to decorate

Preheat the oven to 180°C/Gas 4.

Grease a deep 240 mm loose-bottomed tin and line the base with baking parchment.

Put the butter and both sugars into a bowl and cream together. Beat in the eggs, one by one. Fold in the flour and baking powder.

Toss the ginger, quince cubes and nuts in flour. This will stop them sinking. Gently fold them into the rest of the mixture.

Sprinkle demerara sugar on the top and bake for 1–1¼ hours, or until the cake has risen well.

Check after an hour and place some foil on the top, if it is browning too fast. Leave the cake to cool in the tin for 5 minutes before removing. Transfer to a wire rack until completely cool and sprinkle with icing sugar.

EVERYDAY QUINCE FRUIT CAKE

This makes a small, but very rich cake. A little goes along way. It stores well and can easily be made in advance and kept in an airtight tin.

150 g white self-raising flour
100 g wholemeal self-raising flour
½ teaspoon ground mixed spice
½ teaspoon ground cinnamon
125 g soft butter
125 g soft brown sugar
250 g mixed fruit (including 50 g mixed peel)
1 egg
6 tablespoons milk
125 g poached quince, diced (use the basic poaching method on
*   page 45 with water and lemon)*
demerara sugar, to decorate

Preheat the oven to 180°C / Gas 4.

Line and grease a deep 150 mm loose-bottomed cake tin or insert a ready-made liner for a more professional finish.

Sift the flours and spices into a mixing bowl, add the butter and rub in until the mixture resembles breadcrumbs. Stir in the sugar and dried fruit.

Whisk the egg and milk together and beat into the mixture.

Roll the diced quince in flour to stop the pieces sinking and finally add to the mixture, gently stirring thoroughly.

Put in the prepared tin, sprinkle lightly with demerara sugar and bake 1¼ to 1½ hours. Check after 1 hour and place some kitchen foil over the top if it is browning too fast.

Leave in the tin for 5 minutes, then turn out onto a wire rack to cool.

POSH DODGERS

These biscuits are variations of children's 'Jammy Dodgers'. They are particularly good with the jam on page 56, but any quince jam, or even jelly, will do. The addition of whipped cream makes them a cut above other biscuits.

Makes 24 biscuits.

350 g plain flour
250 g butter, chilled and cut into small chunks
100 g caster sugar
1 egg yolk
quince jam
double cream, stiffly whipped (optional)

Put the flour and butter in a food processor and process until the mixture looks like breadcrumbs. Add the sugar and egg yolk and process until the mixture forms a dough. Turn out onto a floured surface and knead until smooth. Wrap in clingfilm and chill for 30 minutes.

Preheat the oven to 180°C/Gas 4. Grease two baking sheets.

Roll out the dough on a lightly floured surface and cut into 60 mm (2½ inches) circles. Cut a small circle, square or triangle in the centre of half the rounds. Place on the baking trays, allowing about 20 mm (1 inch) between the biscuits so they can spread. Bake for about 12 minutes, until golden brown. Transfer to a wire rack and leave to cool completely.

Spread jam on the whole biscuits and cover with the open ones to form a sandwich. Press the top biscuits down very gently as they have a tendency to break. If you wish you can put a layer of stiffly whipped cream underneath the jam first, but you will need to do this just before you eat the biscuits otherwise they will go soggy.

QUINCELETTES

These little tarts are made with both quince and *membrillo*. They consist of a base layer of pastry, a sweet fruity centre and a soft crowning of sponge. They may appear to involve a lot of stages, but we can assure you they are worth it! They are perfect for afternoon tea, but can also double up as a pudding if you warm them through.

Makes 12 tarts.

shortcrust pastry (you can use ready-made, all-butter pastry or
make your own following the recipe on page 101, depending
on your time and inclination)

Filling
200 g membrillo
2 tablespoons water
1 tablespoon caster sugar

Sponge
125 g soft butter
125 g caster sugar
2 medium eggs
125 g self-raising flour
1 tablespoon hot water
1 large quince poached in water and lemon and diced (use the
basic poaching method on page 45)
12 whole pecan or hazel nuts, for decoration

Preheat the oven to 190°C/Gas 5.

First make the sponge mixture, by creaming the butter and sugar together until light and fluffy. Beat in the eggs one at a time, adding a tablespoon of the flour with the second egg. Fold in the remaining flour, and leave to one side.

Roll out the pastry very thinly on a lightly floured surface. Using an 80 mm (3 inches) pastry cutter, cut out 12 circles. Gently press the pastry circles into a greased tartlet tin.

Add the *membrillo* to the water and sugar and stir over a gentle heat till melted and thoroughly mixed. Spread a generous layer over the base of each tart.

Add the hot water to the sponge mixture. Roll the small pieces of quince in flour to stop them sinking and then gently fold them into the mixture. Spoon it into the pastry cases until three-quarters full, adding a pecan or hazelnut to the top each one. Cook for 15–20 minutes or until golden. Take out of the tin while still warm and cool on a wire rack.

These are particularly good with crème fraîche or the quince custard on page 77.

VICTORIA SPONGE

This is a beautiful cake, with the rosy pink quinces contrasting against the pale sponge. To convert the cake into a pudding use the syrup from the quinces to make the pouring custard on page 77.

225 g soft butter
225 g caster sugar
4 eggs
225 g self-raising flour
2 teaspoons baking powder
2 quinces poached in water and lemon (page 45)
caster sugar, to decorate

Preheat the oven to 180°C/Gas 4. Grease two 200 mm loose-bottomed sandwich tins and line the bases with baking parchment.

Put the butter and sugar into a bowl and cream together. Beat in the eggs, one at a time and then fold in the flour and baking powder. Divide the mixture between the tins and level out.

Bake for about 20 minutes or until well risen and the top springs back when lightly pressed. Leave to cool for a few moments and then turn out onto a wire rack and remove the paper.

Once the cake is cooled spread the quinces out on the bottom layer and put the other layer on top. Dust with caster sugar and serve with the quince poaching liquid.

DRINKS AND LIQUEURS

QUINCE CORDIAL

This is a wonderfully refreshing drink, especially when served with ice on a summer's day. You can dilute the cordial with still or sparkling water, as you prefer.

Makes about 200 ml.

1 large quince
200 ml water, plus about another 300 ml
granulated sugar
lemon juice

Peel the quince and cut into small chunks, removing the core as you go. Put in a saucepan and add the initial quantity of water. Bring slowly to the boil and cover. Simmer gently until the quinces are tender and have turned a pink-orange colour. This will probably take about 40 minutes depending on the fruit.

Pour the contents into a jelly bag and allow the juice to drip through into a bowl. It is easiest if you spoon the fruit into the bag first and then pour the liquid over. Do not squeeze the bag or press the fruit down as this will turn the cordial cloudy. The liquor will take a couple of hours to drip through and can be left overnight. Measure the juice and add an equal weight in grams of sugar for millilitres of juice.

Pour into a clean saucepan and heat gently until the sugar has dissolved. Taste and add lemon juice as necessary. Once the syrup is clear, add the rest of the water, turn up the heat and boil for 10 minutes, so you end up with a thinnish syrup. Remember it will thicken considerably as it cools.

Remove from the heat, skim if necessary and allow to cool slightly before pouring into a bottle.

Serve with still or sparkling water and ice.

You can use the fruit pulp to make the baked custard on page 83.

QUINCE LIQUEUR

This liqueur needs patience; it is simple to make but needs to be left for about six months for the flavour to develop properly.

These quantities will make just over a bottle.

300 g quinces
1 bottle vodka (750 ml)
125 g granulated sugar

Wash the quinces and brush off all the furry down.

Grate the fruit, including the peel and core. This is easiest if you have a food processor as you can cut the quinces in quarters lengthwise and do the whole thing quickly before the fruit has a chance to go brown. The pips are harmful, but only if eaten in large quantities and unless you are going to drink whole bottles of liqueur the amounts here will do you no harm.

Put the grated fruit into a 1 litre preserving jar and sprinkle the sugar on top. Pour on the vodka, ensuring that all the fruit is covered.

Leave in a dark place for 4 months, turning or shaking once a week, or as and when you remember. Taste and add more sugar if necessary. Leave for another 2 months.

Strain into a bottle.

This will keep indefinitely but sediment may form at the bottom, so pour carefully.

QUINCE WINE

Quince wine has been popular in Britain since the eighteenth century, although it was always a 'country' wine, rather than one of fine vintages. In 1872, records show that there were so many quinces in Sussex that, for a short time, wine-making existed on a large scale. This recipe can produce delicious and unusual wine and is well worth the effort, but, like many country wines it is sometimes a little unpredictable. One year we forgot about it and left the bucket under a little-used table for five months. The liquid had turned cloudy as it had been exposed to the air for too long. It was disgusting as wine but, inadvertently, we had made extremely good quince vinegar. Mixed with olive oil, it made a delicious dressing.

The recipe is adapted from one in *The Art of Modern Cookery made plain and easy*, written by Hannah Glasse in 1747.

It is easiest to make this in a plastic bucket with a lid which you can balance on the top; the wine should be covered, but not sealed.

Makes about 2 bottles.

5 quinces
1.2 litres water
225 g granulated sugar
½ lemon, juice and rind
½ thick slice of brown bread, toasted
1 level teaspoon live yeast

Wipe the quinces clean and cut into chunks, discarding the cores as you go. Grate the fruit in a food processor. The original recipe obviously tells you to do it by hand, but this is a laborious task. Put the grated fruit straight into a bowl of water with a little lemon juice to stop it turning brown.

Bring the water to the boil, add the quince and continue to boil for 15 minutes. Remove from the heat.

The recipe then says 'wring hard in a coarse cloth', but wringing out a cloth full of just-boiled fruit is impossible unless you have hands made of asbestos. Put the fruit, a little at a time, into a sieve lined with a jelly bag or piece of muslin and push down hard with the back of a spoon, Put the squashed fruit into a bowl. When you have pressed the pulp once, it should be cool enough to handle. Put it back into the cloth in batches and squeeze as hard as you can to extract as much liquid as possible. There will be a surprising amount.

Remove the lemon rind in wide strips, using a peeler. This way it will be easier to remove later on.

Pour the liquid into a clean bucket and add the sugar, lemon rind and juice. Stir until cold. Rub the toast on both sides with the yeast and add to the liquid. After 24 hours remove the toast. Rest a lid on the top of the bucket and leave for 3 months. It should be kept in a dark place at room temperature. We find under a table or in the bottom of a cupboard best. Larders are too cool, airing cupboards too warm.

Take out the lemon rind, remove any scum gently with a spoon and bottle the wine. If necessary, strain through muslin. There will be a certain amount of gunge at the bottom of the bucket, which you don't want in the bottles, so ladle the wine out, or pour very gently. It is now ready to drink.

RATAFIA

Look in almost any reference book and you will find that each has a different definition of ratafia: a spirit infused with almonds or fruit used to toast a deal or bargain; a nineteenth-century English biscuit; or a French aperitif made from grape juice and brandy. It even appears in Georgette Heyer novels where it is a drink frequently enjoyed by the ladies, but scorned by her gentlemen characters:

> 'We will drink to our bargain first, do you not think?' said the Earl, and picked up a small gilt handbell, and rang it. A lackey came in answer to the bell.
>
> 'You will bring me' – the Earl glanced at Horatia – 'ratafia, and two glasses,' he said. 'And my coach will be at the door within ten minutes.'

'If – if the c-coach is for me,' said Horatia, 'it is only a step to South Street, sir,'

'But I would rather that you permitted me to convey you,' said his lordship.

The butler brought the ratafia himself, and set the heavy silver tray down on a table. He was dismissed with a nod, and went regretfully. He would have liked to see with his own eyes my lord drink a glass of ratafia.

The Earl poured two glasses, and gave one to Horatia. 'The bargain!' he said, and drank heroically.

(Georgette Heyer (1902–1974), *The Convenient Marriage*)

Even the origins of the word are disputed: one school proposing a Latin root, another suggesting it derives from seventeenth-century French Creole. The definition we like best is that it was the liqueur drunk at the ceremonies ratifying European treaties from the fifteenth century onwards. The name could come from the Latin *rata fiat* (let the deal be settled). The liqueur usually consisted of fruit juices, kernels or nuts soaked in a sweetened brandy base, almond flavouring being particularly popular. The danger with using kernels (apricots or peaches) is that when crushed and soaked they produce small amounts of cyanide! The recipe below is a safer option and is based on one in *The Modern Cook*, written by Vincent la Chapelle in 1733.

350 ml quince juice (about 2 large, ripe quinces)
50 g caster sugar
a pinch of cinnamon
1 whole clove
1 whole white or black peppercorn
350 ml brandy
60 g almonds, blanched for 2 minutes and skinned

Cut the quinces into quarters or eighths lengthwise, depending on their size and put through a juicer. The original recipe suggests that you grate the fruit, put it in a cloth and 'squeese it with all your Might', but this is extremely hard work. The number of quinces you will need will vary according to the fruit. If you have much less, or much more, than 350 ml, simply adjust all the other ingredients in proportion.

Put the juice in a pan, bring to the boil and then remove from the heat and allow to cool.

Put the sugar, cinnamon, clove and peppercorn into a pan with 50 ml water and heat gently until the sugar has dissolved. Remove from the heat and allow to cool.

Pour the juice, brandy and sugar solution into a bowl and stir so that the three combine. Add the almonds, if using. Pour into a jar, seal and leave in a cool, dark place for 2–3 months.

Strain the liquid through a muslin cloth. Do not squeeze the cloth as you want the liqueur to be as clear as possible. Finally decant into a bottle and seal; as Vincent la Chapelle puts it, 'Bottles stopped very close' will keep almost indefinitely.

CONFECTIONERY

TUDOR APHRODISIACS

The centre of these chocolates is a variation on *marmelada* or *cotiniat*, which was first imported to England in the fifteenth century. The recipe below is loosely based on one in Gerard's *Herbal*, of 1597. Unlike the marmalade we eat now, this was more of a solid paste and was sold in little wooden boxes or moulded into decorative shapes. It was often eaten at the end of a banquet, possibly accounting for the size of Henry VIII !

Candied fruit came to England at much the same time, from Italy and France. The Italian word *succata* and the French *succade* became suckets, which were sometimes wrapped in gold foil and were often considered to be aphrodisiacs.

These sweets are a combination of the two and are extremely sticky. They are more manageable, and even more indulgent, when covered with dark chocolate.

Makes about a 12–20 chocolates, depending on the size you want.

250 g quinces, peeled, cored and cut into chunks
210 g caster sugar
juice ¼ lemon
100 g small pieces of crystallized fruit (any will do but red fruits
*   such as cherries, or papaya look particularly good)*
100 g good, dark chocolate

Put the quince in a saucepan, cover with water and bring to the boil. Cover and continue boiling until the quinces are soft; this will probably take about 20–30 minutes. Remove the saucepan from the heat, lift out the quinces and mash or purée the fruit.

Measure 50 ml of the cooking liquid into a saucepan. Add the sugar and dissolve over a low heat. Stir until the syrup is clear and then boil without stirring until the syrup is thick and caramel-like. The easiest way to test if it is ready is to spoon some out and drop it into a cup of cold water. It is ready when you can roll it into a ball with your fingers.

Add the quince purée and continue boiling and stirring until the mixture becomes very thick and pulls away from the sides. Remove from the heat, add the lemon juice and candied fruit and mix well.

Line a small baking tin with clingfilm. Pour the mixture into the tin, smooth and put in the fridge to cool. This will probably take a couple of hours, or you can leave it overnight.

Line a baking tray with baking parchment or put a sheet under a wire rack. Cut the mixture into squares. It will squish out of shape as you cut it but this doesn't matter.

Break the chocolate into small pieces and put them into bowl which will fit snugly into a small saucepan. Put a few centimetres of water into the saucepan and simmer gently. Put the bowl into the saucepan, ensuring that none of the water bubbles up into it. Stir the chocolate occasionally until it has completely melted. Remove the bowl from the heat.

Dip the pieces in the chocolate so they are completely coated. This is easiest to do using two forks or cocktail sticks rather than trying to hold the pieces, which gets incredibly messy very quickly.

Place the coated chocolates on the parchment or rack and put in the fridge to set.

QUINCE CHOCOLATES

These chocolates are child's play to make and the *membrillo* centre is unusual and delicious. You can make your own *membrillo* or buy it from Spanish or middle-eastern delicatessens.

Makes about 20 chocolates.

200 g firm membrillo
100 g good dark chocolate (70% is fine)

Cut the *membrillo* into squares and put in the fridge.

Break the chocolate into small pieces and put them into a basin which will fit snugly into a small saucepan. Put a few centimetres of water into the saucepan and simmer gently. Put the bowl into the saucepan, ensuring that none of the water bubbles up into it. Stir the chocolate occasionally until it has completely melted. Remove the bowl from the heat.

Line a baking tray with baking parchment or put a sheet under a wire rack. Dip the *membrillo* squares in the chocolate so they are completely coated. This is easiest to do using two cocktail sticks or forks rather than trying to hold the squares, which gets incredibly messy very quickly.

Place the coated chocolates on the parchment or rack and put in the fridge to set.

Turkish Delight isn't difficult to make, but it is time-consuming. The temperatures and order in which you do things matter, otherwise you are in danger of ending up with pink gloop. The rewards are great though, as the end result is so much nicer than anything you can buy. It should be stored in a wooden or cardboard box rather than a tin.

Makes about 30 pieces.

60 g cornflour
½ teaspoon cream of tartar
425 g caster sugar
½ teaspoon lemon juice
100 g firmly poached quince, cut into small pieces (use the basic
*   poaching method on page 45 with water and lemon; out*
*   of season you can use 100 g* membrillo *cut into small pieces)*

Coating
100 g icing sugar
40 g cornflour

Line a deep baking tray (190x190x30 mm) with oiled clingfilm.

Mix the cornflour and cream of tartar with 430 ml water in a heavy-bottomed saucepan. Bring to the boil, stirring constantly to make sure there are no lumps.

Put the sugar into another saucepan, add 190 ml water and the lemon juice. Bring it to the boil and as soon as the temperature reaches 116°C / soft ball (it should be a pale golden colour), remove it from the heat.

Put the cornflour mixture over a low heat so it is just simmering. Gradually and carefully, add the syrup, beating well so that it is thoroughly incorporated. The mixture will start very gluey and gradually ease to a smooth paste.

Simmer on a very gentle heat for about 2 hours, stirring regularly so the mixture does not stick to the bottom of the pan and burn. The mixture will gradually thicken. When it starts to pull away from the edges add the quince pieces or *membrillo* and stir in evenly.

Pour into the baking tray. Allow to cool overnight at room temperature.

For the coating, mix and sift the sugar and cornflour. Dust a board with the same mixture and turn the Turkish Delight onto it, peeling away the clingfilm. Using an oiled knife, cut into small cubes and roll in the sugar mixture. Store in wooden or cardboard boxes. The Turkish Delight will get sweeter the longer you leave it as it will absorb the sugar.

SHORTCRUST PASTRY

Quantities for the Stained Glass Window Tart

250 g plain flour
125 g chilled butter, cut into chunks
Water, to bind

Quantities to line a 230 mm tin for the Golden Quince Tart and the Quincelettes

180 g plain flour
90 g cold butter, cut into small chunks
Water, to bind

Put the flour into a food processor and blitz briefly so there are no lumps. Add the butter and blitz until the butter and flour are combined and resemble fine breadcrumbs. With the machine running add cold water a spoonful at a time until the mixture forms a dough. Be careful not to add too much water. Wrap the dough in clingfilm and put in the fridge for 30 minutes.

THE BOOKS THAT MADE QUINCES POPULAR

The seventeenth and early eighteenth centuries could be called the Golden Age of the Quince. The fruit was grown in orchards, featured prominently in recipe books and was used for medicinal purposes. Unlike today, everyone would have known what a quince was and how to cook it. This is reflected in the books of the period and many of the recipes we use now date from this time. First, gardening manuals such as *A New Orchard and Garden* by William Lawson showed people how to grow quinces, and herbals by John Gerard and Nicholas Culpeper described their uses. Cookery books followed, with Robert May's *The Accomplisht Cook* and Sir Kenelm Digby's *Closet of Sir Kenelm Digby Opened* each containing a substantial number of recipes for the fruit. This chapter looks at the books which helped bring about the quince's brief period of glory and gives an example on the fruit from each book. Eliza Acton's *Modern Cookery for Private Families* from 1844 is also included, even though it is well outside the quince's golden age, as it has so many excellent quince recipes. *Mrs Beeton's Book of Household Management*, which followed a few years after the second edition of Eliza's book only had two recipes for the fruit.

The books and their authors are only covered briefly, but, we hope, sufficiently to whet the reader's appetite for more. Note that at this time the word 'receipt' was used, rather than 'recipe'. All the books are listed in the bibliography on page 124.

John Gerard is credited as the author of one of the best known herbals. He was born in the mid sixteenth century, had no university training and became a barber-surgeon, an unlikely-sounding combination that was quite common at the time. In 1577 he became gardener to William Cecil and it soon became clear that he was an outstandingly talented plantsman. He was the first gardener to publish detailed records of the plants he grew and many plants are incorrectly dated as first appearing in England in 1596, the year of his list.

The *Great Herball* was published the following year, but should not strictly have been credited to John Gerard. In 1583 Rembert Dodoens, a Belgian botanist had published his collected works. A Dr. Priest was commissioned to translate the work, but died before completing the translation. John Gerard took over, Mrs Gerard advised him on the subjects that would appeal to women readers, he then added some gardening commentary and passed the resulting book off as his own work. He misidentified some of the illustrations and lied about things he had seen, but he had an attractive writing style and the book was an immediate success. In many ways it was a gardener's manual as much as a herbal, with detailed, and mostly accurate, descriptions of plants and information on how to grow them, as well as recipes and advice on health.

Quince Trees

The Quince tree is not great, but growes low, and many times in manner of a shrub: it is covered with a rugged barke, which hath on it now and then certain scales: it spreadeth his boughes in compasse like other trees, about which stand leaves somewhat round like those of the common Apple tree, greene and smooth above, and underneath soft and white: the flours be of a white purple colour: the fruit is like an Apple, saving that many times it hath certain embowed & swelling divisions: it differeth in fashion and bignesse; for some Quinces are lesser and round, trust up together at the top with wrinckles, others longer and greater: the third sort be of a middle manner betwixt both; they are all of them set with a thinne cotton or freese, and be of the colour of gold, and hurtfull to the head by reason of their strong smell; they all likewise have a kinds of choking tast; the pulp within is yellow, and the seed blackish, lying in hard skins as do the kernels of other apples.

The Quince growth in gardens and orchards, and is planted oftentimes in hedges and Fences belonging to Gardens and Vineyards: it delighteth to grow on plain and even grounds, and somwhat moist withall.

The Marmalad or Cotiniat made of quinces and sugar is good and profitable to strengthen the stomack, that it may retain and keep the meat therein untill it be perfectly digested.

WILLIAM LAWSON ON STORING QUINCES

In 1618 *A New Orchard and Garden* with *The Country Housewifes Garden* was published. Written by a clergyman living in Yorkshire, it rapidly became one of the most popular gardening books of the time. The two books were published as one and were meant to be seen as a pair, with frequent references in *The Country Housewifes Garden*, back to the first book. However, they are quite different in tone. *A New Orchard* is a gentle manual, considering the philosophy of gardening and its pleasures, as well as the practicalities of planning and caring for an orchard. *The Country Housewifes Garden* is a more practical book, with clear and simple instructions for creating an attractive and productive garden, and keeping bees. The 1623 edition also included a Treatise by Simon Harward on propagating plants and *The Husband Mans Fruitful Orchard*, which covered gathering and storing the fruit, increasing the yield and 'also the best way of carriage by land or water'. The fruit was clearly meant to be profitable as well as pleasing.

William Lawson may have been a country vicar, but he was broadminded and well-read. He was happy to give away fruit to prevent scrumping; 'Liberality I say is the best fence.' He knew most of the gardening books at the time and deliberately aimed his at gardeners in the harsher north of England, having found that many of the other books were concerned with the more temperate southern or even continental gardens. Even today, his advice is valuable.

Gathering of Quinces

Quinces should not be laid with other fruit, for the sent is offensive both to the other fruit, and to those that keep the fruit or come amongst them: therefore lay them by themselves upon sweet straw, where they may have ayre enough: they must be packt like Medlars and gathered with Medlars.

NICHOLAS CULPEPER'S CORDIAL AND PREPARATION FOR SORE MOUTHS

In many ways Nicholas Culpeper is the opposite of John Gerard, the author of the other herbal considered here. Nicholas was born in 1616, did well at school and excelled at Cambridge. His parents assumed he would become a successful physician or cleric. All these hopes foundered though, as Nicholas fell hopelessly in love and planned to elope. He borrowed £200 from his mother and went to meet his beloved beneath an oak tree. Tragically, it was a stormy night and he arrived to find the tree blasted by lightning and the girl lying dead on the ground. He gave up his studies and, for a time, did nothing.

His parents purchased an apothecary position for him and in 1640 he set up his own business in Red Lion Street, a poor area of Spitalfields in London. Apothecaries were usually ill-educated men and were regarded with scorn by doctors. Nicholas was different to most though, and he was determined to help the poor and improve the status of apothecaries.

In 1652 he published *The English Physician*, and a year later his *Complete Herbal* followed. These books gave ordinary people the ability to improve their health if they wished; no longer did they have to rely on uneducated apothecaries or dishonest physicians. He was convinced that the whole body should be treated and described the occult properties of herbs as well as their medicinal ones. A year later he died, but his books survived. 'Culpeper, the man that first ranged the woods and climbed the mountains in search of medicinal and salutary herbs, has undoubtedly merited the gratitude of posterity.' Dr. Johnson.

Quince trees are described and the benefits of the fruit are then gone into in some detail; it seems as if quinces could be used to cure almost everything from sickness to sore throats in the extract below.

Government and virtues

Old Saturn owns the tree. The fruit has a strong and very pleasing smell, and an austere acid taste. Its expressed juice, taken in small quantities, proves a mild, cooling, astringent stomachic medicine, and is of great efficacy in sickness, vomiting, eructations, and purgings. A grateful cordial, and a lightly restringent syrup, is made by digesting three pints of the clarified juice, with a drachm of cinnamon, half a drachm of ginger, and the same quantity of cloves, in warm ashes, for the space of six hours, then adding a pint of red port, and dissolving nine pounds of fine sugar in liquor, after straining it. And an useful jelly is made, by boiling the juice with a sufficient quantity of sugar, till it attains a due consistence. The seeds abound with a soft mucilaginous substance, which they readily give out to boiling water, rendering it slimy, and almost like the white of an egg. This preparation is an excellent medicine for sore mouths, and may be used with advantage to soften and moisten the mouth and throat in fevers, and other disorders.

Robert May was born in 1588. His father was cook to Sir William and Lady Dormer, who lived at Ascott Park in Wing, Buckinghamshire. When he was ten, Robert was sent to France, where he spent five years, learning his trade and studying French recipes. He then returned to England and completed his apprenticeship in London. Once trained, he went back to Ascott Park and worked with five other cooks, under his father, until 1631. Then he effectively became a freelance chef, working in a number of mostly Catholic, aristocratic, households. He remained in England during the Civil War, working and accumulating recipes and in 1660 his book, *The Accomplisht Cook, or the Art and Mystery of Cookery* was published. This was the first really comprehensive English cookery book, which covered everything from 'The A-la-mode ways of dressing the Heads of any Beasts' to 'the most exquisite way of making pancakes'. Some of the recipes were taken from other sources, but most were Robert's own. He had worked in a number of grand houses and acknowledged in the book that he had been lucky to be able to take advantage of his employers' great wealth. He includes recipes for those whose finances are limited, but makes it quite clear that he was relieved never 'To be confined and limited to the narrowness of a Purse.' The subtitle of the book is *Wherein the whole ART is revealed in a more easie and perfect Method, than hath been publish in any language* and, unlike many other cooks of the time, he was quite prepared to share his knowledge. It is likely that, at the age of seventy-two, he was more concerned with leaving a record of his work than worrying about other cooks using his recipes.

One section of the book is devoted to fruit; *To bake all manner of Curneld Fruits in Pyes, Tarts, or made Dishes, raw or preserved, as Quinces, Wardens, Pears, Pippins, &c.* Their place at the beginning of the list shows how important quinces were at the time and the book has ten recipes for them, including Pickled Quinces, Quince Cream and the selection of pies below, one of which would serve an extremely large dinner party.

To bake a Quince Pye

Take fair Quinces, core and pare them very thin, and put them in a Pye, then put in it two races of ginger slic't, as much cinamon broken into bits, and some eight or ten whole cloves, lay them in the bottom of the Pye, and lay on the Quinces close packed, with as much refined sugar as the Quinces weigh, close it up and bake it, and being well soaked the space of four or five hours, ice it.

Otherways.
Take a gallon of flour, a pound and a half of butter, six eggs, thirty quinces, three pound of sugar, half an ounce of cinamon, half an ounce of ginger, half an ounce of cloves and some rose-water, make them in a Pye or Tart, and being baked stew on double refined sugar.

Otherwise.
Bake these Quinces raw, slic't very thin, with beaten cinamon, and the same quantity of sugar, as before, either in a tart, patty-pan, dish, or in cold butter-paste, sometimes mix them with wardens, pears or pipins, and some minced citron.

To Make a Quince Pye otherways.
Take Quinces and preserve them, being first coared and pared, then make a sirrup of fine sugar and spring water, take as much as the quinces weigh, and to every pound of sugar a pint of fairwater, make your sirrup in a preserving pan; being scumm'd and boil'd to sirrup, put in the quinces, boil them up till they be well coloured, & being cold, bake them in pyes whole or in halves, in a round tart, dish, or patty-pan with a cut cover, or in quarters; being baked put in the same sirrup, but before you bake them, put in more fine sugar, and leave the sirrups to put in afterwards, then ice it.

Thus you may do of any curnel'd fruits, as wardens, pippins pears, pearmains, green quodlings or any good apples, in laid tarts, or cuts.

Sir Kenelm Digby was a scientist, spoke several languages fluently and was a founder member of the Royal Society. He was handsome, clever and popular. He was also a privateer, killed a man in a duel and was accused (almost certainly wrongly) of poisoning his wife. He was born in 1603 and three years later his father, Sir Everard Digby (the most handsome man in England, according to John Aubrey) was hanged, drawn and quartered for his part in the gunpowder conspiracy. Sir Kenelm Digby was restored to his father's estates, but spent much of his life on the continent, sometimes out of choice, at other times banished from England for his Catholic and royalist beliefs. Throughout his life he collected recipes, but never actually arranged them into a book. This was done by his steward, George Hartman, after Sir Kenelm Digby's death in 1665 and in 1669 *The Closet of the Eminently Learned Sir Kenelm Digbie Kt Opened* was published. Here the word 'closet' means a private as opposed to a public apartment. Thus the reader is allowed a glimpse of the author's private life.

Many of the recipes have medicinal benefits, but the overall tone of the book is one of elitism; these are recipes for the rich and aristocratic to enjoy at feasts and banquets. Quinces feature prominently, with a number of recipes for gelly and paste, with variations added from other sources, notably 'White Marmulate, the Queens Way' and next 'My Lady of Bath's Way'. We were pleased to see that his method for testing the setting point of jelly is remarkably similar to ours:

To Make Fine White Gelly of Quinces

Take quinces newly from the tree, fair and sound, wipe them clean, and boil them whole in a large quantity of water, the more the better, and with a quick fire, till the Quinces crack and are soft, which will be in a good half hour, or an hour. Then take out the Quinces, and press out their juyce, with your hands hard, or gently in a press through a strainer, that only the clear liquor or juyce run out, but none of the pap, or solid and fleshy substance of the Quince. (The water they were boiled in you may throw away.) This liquor will be slimy and mucilaginous, which proceedeth much from the seeds that remaining within the Quinces, do contribute to making this Liquor. Take three pound of it, and one pound of fine Sugar, and boil them up to a gelly, with a moderate fire, so that they boil every where, but not violently. They may require near an hours boiling to come to a gelly. The tryal of that is, to take a tin or silver plate, and wet it with fair-water, and drop a little of the boiling juyce upon the wet plate; if it stick to the plate, it is not enough; but if it fall off (when you slope the Plate) without sticking at all to it, then it is enough: and then you put it into flat shallow Tin forms, first wetted with cold water, and let it stand in them for four or five hours in a cold place, till it be quite cold. Then reverse the plates, that it may shale and fall out, and so put the parcels up in boxes.

Note, you take fountain water, and put the Quinces into it, both of them being cold. Then set your Kettle to boil with a very quick-fire, that giveth a clear smart flame to the bottom of the Kettle, which must be uncovered all the while, that the gelly may prove the whiter; And so likewise it must be whiles the juyce or expression is boiling with the Sugar, which must be the finest, that it may not need clarifying with an Egg; but that little scum that riseth at the sides at the beginning of moderate boiling must be scummed away. You let your juyce or expression settle a while, that if any of the thick substance be come out with it, it may settle to the bottom; for you are to use for this only the clear juyce: which to have it the clearer, you may let it run through a large, thin, open, strainer, without pressing it. When you boil the whole Quinces, you take them out, to strain them as soon as their skins crack, and that they are quite soft; which will not happen to all of them at the same time, but according to their bigness and ripeness. Therefore first take out and press those, that are ready first: and the rest still as they grow to a fit state to press. You shall have more juyce by pressing the Quinces in a torcular, but it will be clearer, doing it with your hands: both ways you lap them in a strainer.

JOHN EVELYN'S QUINCE CREAME

John Evelyn was a man of many talents. Born in 1620, most of his school years were spent with his step-grandmother in Sussex. At 17 he went to Balliol College and then the Middle Temple. Here he studied language, philosophy, music and religion, but his curiosity meant that he was frequently diverted. He travelled extensively on the Continent during the years of the English Civil War and married the daughter of the English Ambassador in Paris. Unlike many travellers he used his time productively, learning languages and studying all aspects of the countries he visited. After the Restoration he spent much of his time at Court, acted on public committees and was a founder member of the Royal Society.

His most famous works are his diaries, but he wrote and translated over thirty books, including several on gardening. His book on salads, *Acetaria: A Discourse on Sallets* was published in 1699, unusual for its recommendation that one should always eat salad with meat. He collected a huge number of recipes and his diaries include interesting insights into ingredients he discovered and dinners he attended. His friends were the aristocracy and the intelligentsia, and he describes their houses and lives in detail. He was interested in food, but disapproved strongly of the over-indulgence he frequently saw, both at court and within his own family; his son John drank to excess and he was convinced that his daughter Mary's death from smallpox was largely due to the 'trash and sweetmeats' she ate.

The receipts were written up in a 'large volume bound in decorated calf gilt', which Christopher Driver discovered in the library of Christ Church, Oxford in the 1950s. He typed them up and the 343 receipts were published in 1997 as *John Evelyn, Cook: the Manuscript Receipt Book of John Evelyn*. The recipes were collected from friends and family, both in England and while John was travelling abroad, and range from 'Wormwood Ale' to 'The Making of French Bread'. Many of the places or original authors are credited in the recipe titles: *The manner of making Creame at Soteville by Roane in France Normandy, my Lady Fitzhardings Recet for puffs* and *A riciet for a very light Cake Mrs Cloterbooks way.*

To make Quince Creame

Take an Ale pint of Creame boyle it with mace and cinamon have the yolks of 6 Eggs beaten put them into the cream and when yr creame is pretty thick take it of the fire and stirr in to it 2 Ounces of Quinces parboyled and three spoonfulls of Orenge flower water have some slices of boyled Quince in the bottome of your dish so pour yr creame on them sweeten it to yr taste.

JOHN NOTT'S METHODS FOR STORING QUINCES AND MAKING A PYE

John Nott was a cook who took the unusual step of compiling a dictionary of recipes, *The Cooks and Confectioners Dictionary: Or, the Accomplish'd Housewives Companion* which was published in 1723. He studied the recipes published in the preceding seventy or so years and collected together the best, revising or rewriting where he felt necessary. Robert May's *The Accomplisht Cook* had been published in 1660 and from then on more and more cooks in grand houses had published books of their recipes. Fame was increasingly considered more important than guarding culinary secrets. Grand former employers were frequently listed on the title page, establishing the writer's credentials. In the first edition of his dictionary, John Nott only listed the Duke of Bolton. The second edition, which followed a year later, had a much larger list of nobles.

Little exact detail is known about John Nott's career, but the houses he worked in would have had large kitchens with a fleet of staff to run them. His recipes are for the head cooks of such establishments and many contrast with those of Hannah Glasse, who aimed to make recipes easy and affordable for lesser households.

The recipes were arranged in alphabetical order and included ones by French cooks, such as François Massialot, who had cooked for most of the French royalty and nobility. At the end of the book there is a month by month list of seasonal recipes, followed by instructions for carving, together with a useful glossary. Finally there are directions for setting out desserts in the ornate patterns popular at the time.

There are twenty-two recipes for quinces, the usual marmalades, custards, syrups and tarts, as well as useful information on storing the fruit.

To keep Quinces for Pyes

Wipe them, and put them into a Vessel of Small Beer when it has done working; stop them up close that no Air may get in, and they will keep good all the year.

To make a Quince Pye

Take preserved Quinces, freed from both Parings and Cores, make Syrup with Water boil'd up with fine Sugar; then take as much of it as the Weight of the Quinces you intend to put in your Pye, and put it into a Preserving-pan; boil it, scum it, and then put in your Quinces; let them boil till they be well clear'd, then lay them into your Pye in halves or quarters; make your Pye round with a cut Cover, put in more Sugar, close it up, bake it, and put in your Syrup, and so ice it over.

In 1747 *The Art of Cookery made plain and easy* by 'A Lady' was published. The first edition did not name Hannah Glasse as the author (although she made no secret of the fact) and the title by which it later came to be known, *First Catch Your Hare* was not mentioned anywhere in the text. Unlike Robert May's *The Accomplisht Cook*, this cookery book was written expressly to make money. The address to the reader gives the commendable aim of teaching servants to cook well and economically; 'So in many other Things in Cookery, the great Cooks have such a high Way of expressing themselves that the poor Girls are a Loss to know what they mean', but for Hannah, *The Art of Cookery* was a means to get out of debt.

She had been born illegitimate, in 1708 and although she was brought up in her father's household, he died when she was sixteen. Shortly before, she had married John Glasse. At various stages of his life he may have been a merchant, a debt-collector and a butler, but when he married Hannah he was living on half-pay from the army. Irresponsible and spendthrift, he squandered what money Hannah had, sired eleven children and then died in 1747.

Hannah tried various money-making schemes during the course of her life: first she produced and patented an elixir, known as Dr Lower's Tincture. Then she opened a 'warehouse' in her home and later she set up a clothes shop with her daughter Margaret. *The Art of Cookery* was the most successful venture, but even though it sold well, Hannah was declared bankrupt in 1754 and had to sell the copyright. She wrote two more books, but remained impoverished, spending time in both Marshalsea and Fleet Prisons, before her death in 1770.

Not all the recipes in *The Art of Cookery* are original, but the eight for quinces seem to be Hannah's own. They include fairly standard marmalades, jelly and syrups, and a custard that we have adapted (see page 83). We have also adapted her recipe for wine (see page 93), although it has to be admitted that the results from this can be a little variable. The 'cakes' below are far removed from our afternoon tea sponges, and more like Sir Kenelm Digby's *Gelly*, but are nevertheless interesting.

To make Quince Cakes

You must let a Pint of the Syrrup of Quinces, with a quart or two of Rasberries, be boiled and clarified over a clear gentle Fire, taking Care that it be well skimm'd from time to time; then add a Pound and half of Sugar, cause as much more to be brought to a Candy-height, and pour'd in hot; let the whole be continually stirred about till it is almost cold, then spread it on Plates, and cut it out to Cakes.

ELIZA ACTON'S DELICIOUS BLANCMANGE

Eliza Acton was born in 1799, just over ninety years after Hannah Glasse and by then, for many people, the era of servants and grand estates was over. She was born into a middle class family and, from the age of eighteen, needed to make her living. She spent some time in France, on account of her delicate health, possibly becoming engaged to a Frenchman, while she was there. There were rumours that she had a child with him and then broke off the engagement when he proved himself unfaithful, but none of this is certain, and she returned home alone. Back in England, she first started a boarding school, where she remained for four years and then, in the 1820s, had a selection of her poems published. She went to visit Mr Longman, her publisher, with a view to having more poems published, but he suggested that they would do better with a cookery book. Eliza worked on the book for about ten years and in 1844 *Modern Cookery for Private Families* was published, with a second edition, revised by Eliza, following in 1855. Modern is an apt word for the title as it is regarded by many as the first modern cookery book, being the first one to specify the quantities of the ingredients and the length of cooking time. It marks the end of the era typified by the previous books in this chapter.

The recipes are elegantly written and precise, possibly because of Eliza's earlier teaching and poems. Many of them have witty titles and the inclusion of 'Poor Author's Pudding' and 'The Publisher's Pudding', which 'can scarcely be made *too rich*', make her feelings towards Mr Longman perfectly clear.

The book is aimed at the middle classes, many of whom were becoming increasingly wealthy as a result of the Industrial Revolution. In her preface Eliza points out that these are the people to whom we owe advances in science, art, literature and general civilization and it is important that they are properly fed. For much of her life she lived without servants and cooked her own meals and many of the recipes have notes warning the reader where she went wrong.

Quinces are still popular, but it is no longer assumed that they will come from your own orchard (Sir Kenelm Digby) or that of the local lord (Hannah Glasse). Alongside the usual jelly, paste and marmalade there are recipes for custard (which we have adapted on page 77), juice and blancmanges, one of which Eliza describes as 'delicious', the other as an alternative in winter, when cream is not available. The delicious one is given below.

Quince Blanc-Mange

Delicious

This, if carefully made, and with ripe quinces, is one of the most richly-flavoured preparations of fruit that we have ever tasted; and the receipt, we may venture to say, will be altogether new to the reader. Dissolve in a pint of prepared juice of quinces, an ounce of the best isinglass; next, add ten ounces of sugar, roughly pounded, and stir these together over a clear fire, from twenty to thirty minutes, or until the juice jellies in falling from the spoon. Remove the scum carefully, and pour the boiling jelly gradually to half a pint of thick cream, stirring them briskly together as they are mixed: they must be stirred until very nearly cold, and then poured into a mould which has been rubbed in every part with the smallest possible quantity of very pure salad oil, or if more convenient, into one that has been dipped into cold water.

Obs. – This blancmanger which we had made originally on the thought of the moment for a friend, proved so very rich in flavour, that we inserted the exact receipt for it, as we had had it made on our first trial; but it might be simplified by merely boiling the juice, sugar, and isinglass, together for a few minutes, and then mixing them with the cream. An ounce and a half of isinglass and three-quarters of a pint of cream might then be used for it. The juice of other fruit may be substitute for that of quinces.

Juice of quinces, 1 pint; isinglass, 1 oz: 5 to 10 minutes. Sugar, 10 oz: 20 to 30 minutes. Cream, ½ pint.

THE LOST WORLD OF THE QUINCE:
HEALTH AND BEAUTY

From Classical times up to the nineteenth century there was an abundance of quinces in cookery and health books. Throughout these times cooking and medicine were closely linked as it was not possible to simply take a pill if you felt ill. Many dishes were eaten specifically for their health-giving properties and most people who were rich enough to choose what they ate would have been aware of the properties of the different foods. Quinces were always, quite rightly, regarded as an aid to digestion, but through the years many other claims have been made for them. Some are more rational than others.

One of the more dodgy ideas was a cure for baldness. This was mentioned in the *Natural History* of Pliny the Elder and was widely used during the Middle Ages. At this time many cures were erroneously based on a like-for-like principal and this one was probably based on the fact that the furry down which appears on ripe quinces looks like newly grown hair. The down was mixed with wax and spread on the unfortunate person's head. According to Culpeper in his *Herbal* of 1653 this mixture 'laid as a plaister, brings hair to them that are bald, and keeps it from falling if it be ready to shed.' One cannot help feeling that when the cure was removed any remaining hair might well have been stripped off.

Eating quinces as an aid to digestion was much more sensible and they were often served at the end of banquets for this reason. In 1629 John Parkinson, the Covent Garden Herbalist to the King wrote, 'There is no fruit growing in this Land that is of so many excellent uses as this, serving as well to make many dishes of meate for the table, as for banquets, and much more for the Physicall virtues.' Their health-giving properties were one of the reasons quinces became so popular. London apothecaries even sold quince paste, under the name diasetonia. Culpeper recommends that quince and vinegar 'stirs up a languishing appetite', quince and spices 'comforts and strengthens the decaying and fainting spirits' and quince juice 'is of great efficacy in sicknesses, vomiting, eructations and purgings.'

From medieval times to the seventeenth century quinces were seen as a protection against poisoning and the plague. More bizarrely the furry down was mixed into a paste and spread on plague sores. This wouldn't have done much good, but then nothing was much good against the plague. As a protection against catching it eating quinces was more logical, as the fruit contains vitamin C which would have improved the general health of the person and probably have made them less susceptible to infection. The few sailors who returned to Spain from Magellan's voyage round the world in 1522 were sick and exhausted, but alive, largely thanks to the quinces they had eaten on the voyage.

As we have already remarked, ancient myths regarded the quince as an aphrodisiac and an aid to fertility, largely due to the connection with Aphrodite. And we have already celebrated the ancient claims that a diet of quinces in pregnancy would result in super-intelligent offspring.

Another interesting claim was that they would 'preserveth the head from drunkenness.' This comes from *The Castel of Helth* written in 1541 by Sir Thomas Elyot.

Roast or boil the quinces until they are soft.
Remove the skin and cores and mix the flesh with clarified
honey or sugar.

Unfortunately no information is given regarding how much should be eaten or how soon before drinking it should be taken. Perhaps it depended on how much alcohol you were intending to consume.

Quinces have also been used as beauty products. Even today

quince skin cream is available. The gel which forms when the seeds are soaked in water is valuable as both an anti-inflammatory and a moisturizer. This gel is easy to make by simply soaking the seeds in a jar of water for a couple of weeks. You can use raw seeds but those from cooked fruit form a thicker gel more quickly. When the gel has formed, strain to remove the pips and any remaining bits of fruit. According to Culpeper this gel will cool burns and soothe the sore breasts of women. It can also be used for sore mouths and throats in fevers, but how the gel was administered and how much you took is not made clear. French tradition has it that if you soak the seeds in eau de vie, rather than water, the resulting gel will get rid of wrinkles and give skin the secret of eternal youth.

In France the gel was also used to make hair glossy and in his *Dictionary of Food* of 1873 Alexandre Dumas says it was used by hairdressers.

Remove the seed from cooked quinces.
Wash to remove the flesh, it doesn't matter if a bit remains.
Add sufficient water to easily cover the seeds.
Store in a sealed jar, at room temperature.
The gel should form in a couple of weeks.
Strain the gel, mix with water as necessary and apply to newly-washed hair to make it glossy.

These remedies range from the logical to the ludicrous, but what is certain is that quinces are good for you. They contain a high level of vitamin C and aid digestion, but may perhaps not be so useful in cases of hair loss or drunkenness.

ACKNOWLEDGEMENTS

Firstly, we would like to thank Tom Jaine for having faith in this idea, which is very close to both our hearts. This book has been a long time in the making and we would like to thank all our friends and relatives who have tolerated us talking about quinces too much and serving them too often, in particular Bill, Sophie and Rose Dunster. Tish Clark kindly introduced us to Tom. Deborah Cowles, Sue Gibb, Libby Kerr, Lisa Ashby and Louy Piachaud and, at Books for Cooks, Eric Treuille, Sally Hughes and Camille Rope were brilliant testers and tasters. Simon Darragh told us his interesting, if dangerous, way to core quinces on page 38 and imposed some order on our grammar. We would like to thank Danielle Hanson for her professional expertise with the design of the jacket. As always, we would have foundered long ago without the help and support of our agent Teresa Chris.

We would like to thank the *National Trust Magazine* for allowing us to include the Spiced Quince Upside-Down Pudding on page 76 and Jan Greenland for allowing us to use her recipe for Quince and Apple Shortcake on page 85. We would also like to thank Caroline Clayton for allowing to use the translation of *The Quince* by Shafer ben Utman al-Mushafi made by her father, A. L. Lloyd and Random House Book Group for allowing us to include the extract from *The Convenient Marriage* by Georgette Heyer on page 94.

BIBLIOGRAPHY

Acton, Eliza, *Modern Cookery for Private Families*, Southover Press, 2011.

Beeton, Isabella, *Beeton's Book of Household Management*, S.O Beeton, 1861.

Boardman, John, Griffin, Jasper and Murray, Oswyn, *The Oxford History of the Classical World*, Oxford University Press, 1986.

Cato, *On Farming*, translated by Andrew Dalby, Prospect Books, 1998.

Cuby, Janet, *RHS Plant Finder 2014*, Royal Horticultural Society, 2014.

Culpeper, Nicholas, *The Complete Herbal*, Harvey Sales, 1981.

Dalby, Andrew, *Siren Feasts*, Routledge, 1996.

Davidson, Alan, *The Penguin Companion to Food*, Penguin Books 2002.

Digby, Sir Kenelm, *The Closet of the Eminently Learned Sir Kenelme Digbie Opened*, a transcription of the 1669 edition, edited by Peter Davidson and Jane Stevenson, Prospect Books, 1997.

Dixon Wright, Clarissa, *A History of English Food*, Arrow Books, 2012.

Dumas, Alexandre, *Dumas on Food, Selections from Le Grand Dictionnaire de Cuisine*, translated by Alan and Jane Davidson, The Folio Society, 1995.

Elyot, Sir Thomas, *The Castell of Helth*, 1536.

Evelyn, John, *Acetaria*, a facsimile of the 1699 edition, Prospect Books, 2005.

Evelyn, John, *Directions for the Gardiner and other Horticultural Advice*, edited by Maggie Campbell-Culver, Oxford University Press, 2009.

Evelyn, John, *John Evelyn, Cook*, edited by Christopher Driver, Prospect Books, 1997.

Geddes-Brown, Leslie, *A Book for Cooks: 101 Classic Cook Books*, Merrell Publishers, 2012.

Gerard, John, *Leaves from Gerard's Herball*, arranged by Marcus Woodward, The Bodley Head, 1931.

Glasse, Hannah, *First Catch Your Hare: The Art of Modern Cookery Made Plain and Easy*, a facsimile of the first edition, 1747, Prospect Books, 1995.

Graves, Robert, *The Greek Myths*, Penguin Books, 2011.

Grigson, Jane, *Jane Grigson's Fruit Book*, Penguin Books, 2000.

Heyer, Georgette, *The Convenient Marriage*, Cornerstone, 2013.

La Chapelle, Vincent, *The Modern Cook*, 1733.

Lane Fox, Robin, *Better Gardening*, R. & L., 1982.

Lawson, William, *A New Orchard and Garden with The Country Housewifes Garden*, a facsimile of the 1656 edition (first printed in 1618), Prospect Books, 2003.

McMorland Hunter, Jane, *The Tiny Garden*, Frances Lincoln, 2006.

McMorland Hunter, Jane and Kelly, Chris, *For the Love of an Orchard*,

Pavilion, 2010.

May, Robert, *The Accomplisht Cook*, a facsimile of the 1685 edition (first printed in 1660), Prospect Books, 1994.

Nott, John, *Cooks and Confectioners Dictionary*, a facsimile of the 1726 edition, Lawrence Rivington, 1980.

Palter, Robert, *The Duchess of Malfi's Apricots and Other Literary Fruits*, University of South Carolina Press, 2002.

Petronius, *The Satyricon*, translated by P. G. Walsh, Oxford University Press, 1996.

Pliny the Elder, *Natural History*, translated by John F. Healey, Penguin Books, 1991.

Roach, F. A., *The Cultivated Fruits of Britain*, Blackwell, 1985.

Willes, Margaret, *The Making of the English Gardener: Plants, Books and Inspiration 1560–1660*, Yale University Press, 2013.

Wilson, C. Anne, *The Book of Marmalade*, Prospect Books, 1999.

INDEX OF RECIPES

afternoon tea, 85
    everyday quince fruit cake, 87
    ginger and quince cake, 86
    posh dodgers, 88
    quince and apple shortcake, 85
    quincelettes, 89
    victoria sponge, 90
apple pancakes, and quince, 78
apple, and quince shortcake, 85

bake a quince pye, to, 109
baked quinces, 41, 42
    to bake a quince pye, 109
biscuits, posh dodgers, 88
black-eyed beans, and buttered
    quince, marinated chicken with,
    64
blanc-mange, quince, 117
buttered quince, and black-eyed
    beans, marinated chicken, 64

cake, ginger and quince, 86
    victoria sponge, 90
    quince, savoury, 69
cakes, to make quince, 116
camel driver's feast, 43
casserole, hot lightning, 67
charlotte, Sally's, 74
chestnut mushrooms, with pork fillet
    and quince, 61
chickpea tagine, and lamb with
    couscous, 62
chocolate tart, and quince curd, 82
chocolates, quince, 99
confectionery, 97
    quince chocolates, 99
    shortcrust pastry, 101
    Tudor aphrodisiacs, 97
    Turkish delight, 100

cordial, Nicholas Culpeper's for sore
    mouths, 106
    quince, 91
coronation quinces, 42
couscous with poached quinces, 50
    with lamb and chickpea tagine,
    62
creame, to make quince, 113
curd, quince, 58
    quince and chocolate tart, 82
custard, pouring, 77
    quince pots, 83

drink, indulgent with poached
    quinces, 51
drinks and liqueurs, 91
    quince cordial, 91
    quince liqueur, 92
    quince wine, 93
    ratafia, 94
duck breasts, with quince sauce, 60

easy trifle with poached quinces, 51

fruit cake, quince, everyday, 87

gelly, of quinces, to make a fine
    white, 110
ginger poached quinces, 49
    and quince cake, 86
goat's cheese, tart, and quince, 66
golden quince, tart, 72

hot lightning, casserole, 67

ice-cream, 73

jam, quince, 56
jelly, quince, 57

keep quinces for pyes, to, 114

lamb, and chickpea tagine with couscous, 62
liqueur, quince, 92

marinated chicken, with buttered quince and black-eyed beans, 64
membrillo, preserve, 54
mushrooms, chestnut, with pork fillet and quince, 61

Nicholas Culpeper's cordial for sore mouths, 106

oven-poached, vanilla quinces, 48

pastry, shortcrust, 101
pheasant, with quince, 63
poached quinces, 44
    ginger, 49
    in easy trifle, 51
    indulgent drink, 51
    spiced, 47
    with couscous, 50
    with salad, 50
pork chops, spanish, with quince sauce, 68
    fillet, with quince and chestnut mushrooms, 61
posh dodgers, biscuits, 88
pots, quince, 83
pouring custard, 77
preserves, 52
    curd, 58
    membrillo, 54
    quince jam, 56
    quince jelly, 57
    spiced preserved quinces, 59
pudding, surprise, 75

upside-down,spiced quince, 76
pye, to bake a quince, 109
    to make a quince, 114
pyes, to keep quinces for, 114

quince blanc-mange, 117
quincelettes, tarts, 89

ratafia, spirit, 94
recipe ideas for poached quinces, 50

salad with poached quinces, 50
sauce, quince, with duck breasts, 60
    with spanish pork chops, 68
savoury dishes, 60
    duck breasts with quince sauce, 60
    hot lightning, 67
    lamb and chickpea tagine with couscous, 62
    marinated chicked with buttered quince and black-eyed beans, 64
    pheasant with quince, 63
    pork fillet with quince and chestnut mushrooms, 61
    quince and goat's cheese tart, 66
    savoury quince cakes, 69
    spanish pork chops with quince sauce, 68
savoury, quince cakes, 69
shortcake, quince and apple, 85
shortcrust pastry, 101
sore mouths, Nicholas Culpeper's cordial, 106
spanish pork chops, with quince sauce, 68
spiced poached quinces, 47

spiced quince upside-down pudding, 76
spiced quinces, preserved, 59
spirit, ratafia, 94
stuffed quinces, 41
suprise pudding, 75
sweet dishes, 71
    golden quince tart, 72
    ice-cream, 73
    pouring custard, 77
    quince and apple pancakes, 78
    quince curd and chocolate tart, 82
    quince pots, 83
    Sally's charlotte, 74
    spiced quince upside-down pudding, 76
    stained glass window tart, 71
    surprise pudding, 75
    tarte tatin, 80

tagine, chickpea and lamb with couscous, 62

tart, chocolate, and quince curd, 82
    goat's cheese, and quince, 66
    golden quince, 72
    stained glass window, 71
    tarte tatin, 80
tarte tatin, 80
tarts, quincelettes, 89
trifle, easy with poached quinces, 51
Tudor aphrodisiacs, confectionery, 97
Turkish delight, 100

upside-down pudding, spiced quince, 76

vanilla quinces, oven-poached, 48
victoria sponge, cake, 90

white gelly of quince, to make a fine, 110
wine, quince, 93